MW00781478

FRONT PORCHES, CLOTHESLINES, AND BARBED WIRE FENCES

John Pelham

PublishAmerica
Baltimore

ISBN: 978-1-60749-789-9 (softcover)
ISBN: 978-1-4489-2853-8 (hardcover)
PUBLISHED BY PUBLISHAMERICA, LLLP
www.publishamerica.com
Baltimore

Printed in the United States of America

CONTENTS

FOREWORD

In case you haven't noticed lately, "country" is back in. Everywhere you look folks are running "back to the country" in droves. Those of us who were privileged to have grown up beyond the skirts of town understand this urge, but what is it for which they seek? What is it that they hope to leave behind? And, what is it with which they hope to replace it? More importantly, will they like what they find, once they get there, as much as they had envisioned?

The idea behind this book is that the concept, "country" is many things to many people. It is, of course, something different for those who live/grew up "out there" from those who live and/or grew up in more urban climes. It is even different for those who grew up in the country-some of us, like me, thought it was a hard-working, sometimes lonely, "long-way from town" way of life. If you're an only child like me, you had no siblings to help with the chores, so all the work that Mom and Dad didn't want (or have time) to do fell on you. Looking back on it, I'm sure the magical, serene view I have of it now was sure not how I viewed it back then!

However, there are other, different, perspectives: between those who grew up in rural areas in different eras; those who grew up in rural areas in vastly different geographical areas; and, finally, we should all recognize the differences between the subjective and more objective views of country life. Each of these perspectives will be approached in this book. First, several of the poems and short stories will address, both subjectively and objectively, the nuances of the author's life as a "country boy." Additionally, poems and short stories are written from the perspective of two family members (my father and mother-in-law) and from the perspectives of friends who grew up in a "different country." geographically and historically. Readers are

5

invited to notice the similarities and differences in lifestyles as they go from reflections of life in rural New Jersey, to Missouri, Arkansas, Oklahoma, and Texas. It's pretty obvious that there are many similarities and some regional differences-but far fewer than one would expect. Similar themes are found throughout their writings and remembrances-hard work, making do with what one had, finding fun where and however possible, education, transportation, and family life. In all instances where I have included excerpts and/or poems from these individuals, I have done so with their express permission.

Finally, like the first book, this one would not have been possible without the help and guidance of lots of people. While I can't name them all here, I'll start again with my wife, Rita-my most trusted advisor/proofreader/critic and salesperson. Thanks also go to many friends and neighbors who provided poems and stories for the book and, most of all to my wonderful story-telling mother-in-law, Mrs. Norene Letbetter for her insightful look at country life early in the twentieth century. I'll again thank Mrs. Jean Carmichael for the wonderful artwork that serves as the book's cover. Finally, my thanks to all the folks at PublishAmerica for their help, without which all of this would have been confined to my computer.

MY LIFE "ON THE FARM"

As I considered how I would present my personal reflections on country life, I decided to resurrect a poem that I had written several years ago. It was the first "serious" poem I had ever written. As you will see, it summarized my experiences of life on the family farm I shared with my parents from my third year in school until I graduated from Whitney High School in 1956. Instead of simply reproducing it here, however, I have added comments and additional information following each verse. I hope these additions help to understand my feeling about some of the best years of my life (although I certainly didn't always understand or appreciate that). Here, then, are my reflections of life on the farm:

> *If you're like me, you can recall*
> *where you spent your childhood*
> *Where everything looked, sounded,*
> *and smelled real good.*
> *For me, that was the Tarver community*
> *Not too far from the little Texas town of Whitney.*
> *We kept a few of every species:*
> *cows, hogs, chickens and goats,*
> *Planted a little bit of corn and a whole lot of oats.*
> *But I'll tell you I've never been as blue*
> *and plumb low-down*
> *As when Momma and Daddy sold out and moved to town!*

The Tarver community, where our little farm was located, was about three miles outside the town of Whitney, whose population in 1950 was less than 1,000. Only about four or five families lived

7

within a two or three mile radius around the old Tarver School building—long since abandoned as a school and turned into a hayshed. We moved to the farm right after my Dad was transferred to the William Cameron Lumber Yard in Hillsboro in 1946. While I was only eight years old and in the third grade, I remember vividly the first time I saw the place—it was horrible! As I describe it in the next verse, it was an old house—built probably around the turn of the century and built with square nails, so it can safely be said that we were in the country! Daddy loved animals! He stocked a few of almost all two-legged feathered and four-footed haired animals known to mankind, from guineas (those loud-mouthed feathered watchdogs) to hogs, cattle, sheep, goats, and a horse. In addition, we raised a variety of crops, mostly for livestock feed. Fortunately, his dual role as lumberyard manager precluded his becoming a "full-fledged" row-crop farmer (thus avoiding, with only a few exceptions, our having to chop and pick cotton, chop and pull corn, etc.).

When we first moved to the farm,
we didn't know what we'd face
There was an outdoor toilet
and the only heat was a double fireplace.
(There may be some who don't know
'bout a double fireplace, I reckon.
It's one that sits between two rooms
and sends out heat in both directions.)
Daddy had the REA run a line down about a mile and a quarter
So we could have lights, a pump and running water.
We dug tanks, built a bathroom
and barns that were dry and warm
That was several years before Momma and Daddy sold the farm.

My Dad, as was typical of men his age and background, had grown up in a home without indoor toilet facilities, electricity, or other "luxuries." He determined that he wouldn't live in that kind of place again, so he had the Rural Electrification Administration (REA) office in Itasca, about 50 miles away, run a line down to our house, a distance of about half a mile. Even though that gave us the luxury of living with electricity, we still had the outdoor toilet facilities (a two-holer out by the hog pen) and only the fireplace for heat. Those of you who have lived with those know how uncomfortable they both can be in the cold months of winter—even if, like me, you grew up in the warm climes of Texas or the South. Our house, built around the turn of the twentieth century, wasn't insulated and the two layers of wallpaper on the walls didn't do too much to turn the wind on those cold winter nights— especially in my bedroom, which was a couple of rooms away from the fireplace. Thank Goodness for flannel bed sheets!

We did a lot of building around the place—my Dad was an accomplished carpenter, draftsman and lumberman. In addition to all the outside buildings, we also did a lot of work on the house itself. We eventually installed a water line into the house so that we could have an indoor bathroom and a much nicer kitchen. An underground butane tank made it possible for us to have heat other than from the fireplace and I got my own heater. How great that was! Overall, it wasn't much if you happened to see it from the perspective of "city life," but it was home to us.

When you're young in the country
all spry and full of pep
You never even notice
that you might be a mite out of step
With the rest of the world and all its citified notions.
I remember going to Fort Worth and causing quite a commotion.
With stock loaded to the top of the boards,
I'd go to town in that "Row Binder" all yeller as a punkin'.
All them city folk eyein' me like I was a country bumpkin.
But those folks in town
never had the grace and charm
That we had before Momma and Daddy sold the farm.

Life on the farm with my Dad wasn't easy. He was a real task-master (more on this later) and expected my Mother and me to pull our share of the load, but the best part of that life was taking livestock to the Fort Worth Stockyards when we had animals ready to go to market. As a younger boy, I always enjoyed going up there with my Dad. We got to eat a hamburger at a little café there in the Stockyards and I got to watch the yardmen "work" the animals. What a treat! However, the fun I had as a youngster was magnified when I became old enough to go on my own. I felt about ten feet tall when I was allowed to go up there by myself—that is, until I went up the first time. We had a ¾-ton, 1950's-era International pickup—YELLOW—that didn't run well. Sometimes, I'd have hogs or sheep stacked two-deep in that thing—bawling, bleating, and oinking for all they were worth. As I would ease up to a stoplight on North Main, it was all I could do to keep that truck running 'til the light changed. It was pretty clear to me that every eye in Fort Worth was aimed right at me and all the people behind those eyes were saying under their breath, "Look at that. What a country bumpkin that kid is!" I was mortified, but the recognition that kind of responsibility got me among my peers made the whole thing worth it—almost.

Why, I can remember
when kids from town wanted to come out
To my house and run around
and scream and shout.
See, we could do whatever we wanted way out there.
Nobody around to hear us 'cept the stock and they didn't care.
We could do most anything, so long as we didn't get caught;
Smoking cedar bark, walkin' the rails
and doing lots of things we hadn't ought.
'course we didn't think we was doing anybody any harm .
We had lots of fun out there before Momma and Daddy sold the farm.

As envious as I was of my "town friends," with their easy life and their nearness to the picture show and other accoutrements of "urbanity," when it came time for them to come out to see me, I was in "hog heaven." All the things we could get into out there! We had a railroad track that divided our place and it was great fun to go down and wave at the trains as they came through, dream about where they were going and wish we could go with them, and harvest the flattened penny we had put on the rail before the train came along. The rail line also gave us the opportunity to walk the rails, either to see what we might find along the way or to walk it all the way into town.

The seclusion of growing up on the farm also lent itself to other sources of fun. My cousin, Robert, and I loved to sing the songs of Hank Williams, Lefty Frizzell, Earnest Tubb, and other "hillbilly" singers of that era. Out there, we could do that at the top of our lungs and only the animals could protest. The fact that they didn't, had less to do with our abilities than to their inattentiveness, I guess. In addition to our auditioning for the Grand Old Opry, we also did a few other things that were innocuous by today's standards, but we thought they were really pushing the envelope of acceptability. One of those things was our propensity to smoke anything—coffee, grapevines, and cedar bark, among others. Anything of that nature that we tried had the same effect as lighting a blowtorch and pointing it down our throats—HOT and ACRID! With all that, though, we never did anything destructive or harmful to ourselves or the property and stock around the place, so I guess we could be excused of our little peccadilloes.

I'll write one verse each about my Mom and Dad
Since they're both gone, more than that'll make me too sad.
My Dad was 'bout the hardest workin' so-and-so I ever knew
He worked hard and expected
everybody 'round him to work like a dog, too.
I've always said this about him and his love of the land

He managed a lumberyard in town
so he could call himself a farmerman.
The tales I could tell 'bout that man could fill a book
But the one 'bout our buying the bull on Sunday
gives a pretty good look.
Now, doing' stuff like that on the Sabbath
wasn't something to be done,
But we did one Sunday morning and brought him on home.
The next morning we got up
to look at our red and white bounty
But that ole' varmint wasn't anywhere to be found
in all of Hill County!
Daddy even asked a fortuneteller
whose words brought even more alarm.
Needless to say, he never did that again
as long as Momma and Daddy owned the farm!

Elsewhere in this book, I tell some stories about my Dad and some of his personality traits. Most notably, he was what we would call today, a Type A kind of guy. The word "workaholic" also fits. Whether you were a family member or one of the hired hands, whether you were working for him at the lumberyard or on the farm, he expected the most out of everyone. If you weren't busy, he'd find something for you to do. At the lumberyard, if you weren't loading or unloading lumber, sheetrock, cement, etc., he'd find that the office and showroom area needed a vigorous sweeping, mopping and straightening up. Of course, on the farm there was never a lack of things that needed to be done, so it was there that I was most involved—at least 'til I became old enough to work part-time at the yard. The story about the missing bull typifies his "bullheadedness."

My Dad and Mother were active members of the King Memorial Methodist Church in Whitney and he was one of the trustees (what Baptists might call a deacon or others might call an elder), so there were things you could do on the Sabbath and things you were NOT to do. Buying and selling livestock fit easily into the latter category, but when you work at the lumberyard six days a week, sometimes Sunday was the only day in which to do certain things. The Gollihar Hereford Ranch was about ten or twelve miles north of Whitney and that's where Dad bought all our bulls and where I bought my first registered Hereford cattle. Dad had made a deal with "Mr. Wiley" to buy a nice young bull and so we went out there one Sunday morning AFTER CHURCH to pick him up—knowing, of course, the sanctions that might befall an infidel doing such work on the Sabbath. We brought him home and unloaded him in a little patch just outside the front door of our home. Well, the Devil himself must have been watching as we unloaded him and knew exactly where he was and where the low place in the fence was because when we got up the next morning the rascal was GONE—not just out of the patch, but out of any way of finding him. Daddy, who would never have thought about doing such a thing under ordinary circumstances, even went to a fortune teller who gave him several "leads," none of which turned up "hide nor hair" of that bull! Bull buying and conveying never again took place on the Lord's Day.

My Mother, it's safe to say, and has been said
Was the real strength of the family (but don't tell my dad).
On top of all the work she did 'round the home place,
She kept the yard books
and welcomed everyone with a smiling' face.
As I said before, if you worked for my Dad,
you worked real hard
Whether it was at home, on the farm, or at the lumberyard.
That was true for all of us, Mother included, too.
Daddy was always coming up with something for us to do.
Painting' kerosene on mesquites to kill 'em in the heat,
Handling' peanuts seven times or more

so they would make sheep feed cheap!
She never complained and maintained her unique charm
Right up to the day Momma and Daddy sold the farm.

My Mother was as near a pioneer woman as any woman I ever knew. Born and raised on a poor blackland farm, she was used to hard work. She was also as close to a saint as any woman I ever knew. She worked right beside my Dad on the farm and at the lumberyard as well. She was the bookkeeper, but much more. She was generally the first person you met when you came in and, just as likely as not, it was her who got whatever it was the customer wanted—whether it was a piece of lumber, a bucket of paint, or a piece of glass which she had to cut to size. As tired as she was, as much as she might have wished to be home doing her housework, I never heard her complain, let alone talk back to my Dad. That latter trait made her saintly in my eyes! A couple of examples of how she exemplified that trait in the face of what I would call (and did under my breath) "make work" perpetrated by Daddy follow.

Some of our pastures were becoming overrun with mesquite trees. For those who don't know, the mesquite tree is one of the most noxious plants you can have in pastures. Along with cactus and cedar, it spreads like wildfire and saps the soil of every drop of moisture in it, making the growing of grass virtually impossible, so, getting rid of the stuff is not only necessary and costly, but continuous. Dad had a very cost-effective method of killing it—paint each tree trunk of any size (usually four inches or larger) with coal oil up about 12 inches and let the liquid run down and kill the tap root. Now, that is an efficient and effective kill method, but only cost-effective if you have free labor available. He did—himself, my Mother, and me. The biggest rub to it was that it was only effective if you did it in the heat of SUMMER!

One other interesting summer job Dad got us into was when he planted a field above our house in peanuts. Only about 12-15 acres, the soil was just right and we made a really good crop of peanuts. The only thing about it was that we didn't need them for anything other than sheep feed—but feeding them the peanuts in their untreated form wasn't feasible. They had to be turned into hay. I won't bore you with all the details, but, following his plowing them up, we (my Mom, cousin Robert, and I) handled those peanut vines three times before we got them into the barn. Then, the bailing, stacking, loading, unloading, grinding, and feeding the ground peanut hay to the sheep made it the most expensive feed we ever fed—that is, if our labor had been worth anything! Needless to say, the feed was extremely high in protein content and the sheep really liked and really did well on it, but it was the most expensive protein they ever got. Thank Goodness, Dad never got the itch to raise peanuts again!

When I look back on those carefree days
I get nostalgic for the good ole' country ways.
Of doing' for ourselves and for the others around
And helping out our neighbors when their times were down.
Like when the weather was ugly and storms were bad
They'd come to our cellar—the only one to be had.
And, if our cow was fresh and theirs was dry
They'd borrow from us to drink and make their pie.
And you can bet when the shoe was on the other foot
We'd come to them with our hands out and they'd follow suit.
Times, though, have changed and life has lost a bit of its charm
Since the days before Momma and Daddy sold the farm.

I think one of the characteristics that people say about country folks is that they are friendly and they care about their neighbors. Many stories are told about folks helping their neighbors rebuild barns and houses after fires and storms have ravaged their buildings. If you're in need of a plow or other farm tool, if your neighbor has one, you can bet they'll loan it to you. Well, that's the way it was in the Tarver community. We had the only "storm cellar" in the community and when the spring storms came, we could expect company on a regular basis. The neighbor lady was as afraid of storms as my Mom was, and she would bring her husband (who usually walked around outside until the rain got so bad he had to come in) and her daughter every time the clouds got bad. Although we never had a tornado, she was consumed with the fear that one was just down the road every time the lightning would start.

Thankfully, just as we gave to them in that way, they gave back in any way they could when we needed it. The man in the family worked on the railroad and when crossties had to be replaced anywhere near our place, he'd tell Dad where the old ones were and, more often than not, would help us load them and bring them back to our place to use in building fences and barns.

I've got lots of memories, some good and a few bad
Of my life on the farm and the times we had.
My cousin Robert and I rode the range far and wide
On Cricket and Oscar and several other old hides.
They were like Kentucky Derby winners to us, though
'cause they got us in style where we wanted to go.
If we'd been in Montana or somewhere in the Old West
We couldn't have been happier 'cause we had the best.
That's the way things were looking back through the warm
Rays of memory before Momma and Daddy sold the farm.

These last two verses don't need much elaboration. Call it nostalgia if you want, but they merely convey what growing up "out there" meant to me and how they seem now as I look back through the mist of time and space. It's true when they say, "you can't go back," but it did seem to be important for me to visit one last time. I can't say I enjoyed the visit, but it was important to get some closure on that chapter of my life, so long ago written, but not quite finished. It was, at least, bittersweet. The mesquites were back in even greater numbers and force than before we painted them with coal oil. The barns we built with used cross ties and old lumber and corrugated tin were old and falling down. The trees in which and under which I'd played were not as big as I'd remembered them being, but I think that was more a function of my boyhood perspective than from anything subsequent owners had done or not done. Just as not every book ends on a pleasant note, but does bring closure to the story, this visit did this for me. However, just as it sometimes does when we reach that "certain age," it's much more pleasant for me to remember my life on the farm as it was then, not as it would be if I were there now.

Well, I went back to the farm here a while ago
To see again the home I used to know.
It wasn't the same; the trees not as big or the grass as green
As I'd long remembered them bein'.
But, the house was there and the barns we'd built,
The mesquites and cactus we didn't quite get kilt.
The tanks we'd dug and the trees where I'd played
Were still there along with the water lines we'd laid.
The memories were sharp and the feelings were warm
Of the place we lived 'til Momma and Daddy sold the farm.

Well as is so often the case, that wasn't the last time I went to the old farmstead. A few months ago, I went out there again. Suffice to say, it was even worse than it was in the verse above. Some guy "from the city" had bought it, razed **everything** and turned it into a pasture for his cattle. Try as hard as I could, I couldn't find the slightest hint that anything had ever been built on the property; not a board, not a nail, not anything, except the cellar where we had spent so many Spring nights long years ago. Needless to say, it almost made me sick at my stomach and I came home and wrote the following, last verse:

17

Again, I went to see the place once more
Not knowing what I'd see, but pretty shore
It wouldn't be like I'd remembered it bein'
But, I certainly wasn't ready for the sight I was seein'.
The old house was gone—not a board or nail in sight.
I looked for the barns—all gone—something just wasn't right!
Even the tank we'd dug—filled in and covered with brush
All the things we'd built—all gone—my heart was crushed.
But, as I looked further, I realized they hadn't eliminated everything;
There's' the old cellar where we'd spent so many nights of Spring.
Needless to say, I won't go back. I'll just have to remember the charm
Of how it all looked before Momma and Daddy sold the farm.

FRONT PORCHES, CLOTHESLINES, AND BARBED WIRE FENCES

Been to the country lately?
I mean, out where the real people live.
Where dogs or guineas announce your visit
Where people will give what they have to give.

If you haven't been out there lately
I'll tell you of a little you've missed
Just remember as we go through the following
You can certainly add more to the list.

They don't make front porches anymore
Not like the ones we used to know
Where the gentle evening breezes
Each evening, gently blow.

Now, out away from the house
There's what they call "the yard fence"
We had one at the house I grew up in
But, I haven't had one ever since.

Most times, it was just for the show
But, if you had livestock, it was more
It kept cows and other critters
From coming in yore front door.

Depending on what kind of stock you had
The fence was usually woven or barbed wire
Sometimes, it you were really rich
You might have pickets, two feet or higher.

You probably will find some other things
Out in the back yard in those days back then
Among others, we always had a clothesline,
A cellar, barns, and chicken and hog pens.

Even though many people had clotheslines
It wasn't all that uncommon to find
Clean-washed clothes hanging
Out on the top of the fence line.

One thing I've noticed lately
Has to do with entrance gates
Where ours was a barbed wire pull-tight
I see lots nowadays that are real fashion plates.

In fact I see lots of 'em
As I ride down the road
That are just down-right ostentatious
…and, they must have cost quite a load.

Why do people do that
After all, it's just about putting on "face"
They sure don't make the place more home
They add style, but not much grace.

Well, that's just what's happening
In the "country" these days
Lots of folks with lots of money
Are trading the city for "country ways."

I expect there's lots of things
We won't see from folks of their kind
They won't have dogs under the front porch
Nor clothes hanging on the yard fence line.

MILKIN'

Ever' mornin' 'bout six o'clock
here'd come my dad and he'd say:
"I'll give you one more shake and if you're not awake,
there'll be the Devil to pay."

Why he came so early,
the reason I never quite got
'cause, without a doubt, it'd be so dark out
you couldn't see your way to the lot.

It was time to milk,
the Jersey cow just couldn't wait;
her calf was bawlin' and she was callin';
however I felt, I just couldn't be late!

Off to the barn I'd go
mumblin' all the way
wonderin' why, with sun yet not in the sky,
it couldn't wait 'til later in the day.

That was just my Dad's way
"Later" wasn't a word he used.
"Now" was his style; he didn't accept, "after while"
It really didn't matter that I felt so abused.

So, to the barn I went
with milk bucket in hand,
let the calf in, maybe, luckily, then
the cow would quietly stand.

Then, the milking would start
and the real fun would begin.
I'd let the calf suck and with a little luck,
the milk would start to flow then.

But, as sure as you're born
and Jesse James was a train robber,
I was faced with a curse, 'cause as the calf nursed,
there was just bound to be lots of slobber.

Did I mention the cockleburs?
No? How could I have overlooked that?
They'd be all in her tail and without fail
around it'd come in my face—KERSPLAT!!!

Well, that hurt like fire;
made me madder'n an old wet hen.
I'd just get over that, down again on the stool I'd sat
ready to begin again and then…

Sometime during the milkin',
you could bet sure as shootin'
into the bucket she'd step, nothin' I could do to help.
And the milk with lot-dirt it was pollutin'

There I was, wasn't nothin' I could do
but reach in the bucket and take out
anything not white. I know it wasn't right
but I had to bring back milk, no doubt.

Heck, it didn't seem to matter much.
After all, we strained it through a cloth rag.
So, I felt with surety, we got rid of the impurity
Thinkin' back about it now, I want to gag.

The worst thing that could happen
was for the cow to kick the bucket upside down.
All the milk would spill, I had a notion to kill
that hussy and buy our milk in town.

That woud'a taken care of two things
of which I'd had just about enough:
I'd got rid of that chore, I liked bought milk more.
'cause to tell the truth: knowin' what was in that bucket,
I just never would drink that filthy stuff!

CROSSTIMBERS FARMING

Cattle skinny as a rail
Cotton too spotty to bale
Fences startin' to fail
Mesquite trees sappin' the ground.
Johnson grass takin' over th' place
Cactus is winnin' the race
Tryin' to give good grass some space
I'm wonderin' if this decision was sound.

I've tried as hard as I could
To make this bad place good
Now, I'm wonderin' if I should
Pull the plug and go on back to town?
But, I just can't go
I love this old place so
It just don't seem right to let go
And, that's why I'm feelin' so down.

My F-12's in the barn
Can't even plow my nubbin corn
Why didn't somebody warn
Me that this wasn't gonna be a success?
Pinkeye's infected my bull
Grasshoppers are getting' full
Rain's in a five-year lull.
I'm second-guessin' myself, I confess.

This ground's so sorry
It makes me worry
If I should be in any hurry
To plant another crop of corn.
The last crop I tried
Got droughted out and died
My wife just sat down and cried
Was this the life to which she was born?

Pasture's burnt brown
Part of the back fence is down
The banker just turned me down
For a short-term plantin' loan
The stock tank's bone dry
Buzzards' circlin' the sky
I 'spect I know why
I've been hearin' ole Bessy moan.
Just don't know if I can make it
Don't even know if I can take it
There's this feelin', I can't shake it
Sometimes, I think losin's gonna win
Then, a little gleam of hope
Fate just threw down a rope
And I think, nope,
I'll put off a while givin' in.

This is Crosstimbers farmin'
Bad news comes without warnin'
Sometimes it's much less than charmin'
But, it's the life we've chosen to live.
So, we'll keep our heads high
Keep pressin' back a deep sigh
Ever' day gettiin' up to give it a try
Pledgin' to give it everything we've got to give!

HALLOWEEN IN WHITNEY

Someone asked at a party the other night
What's your favorite holiday and why.
That set me to thinkin' 'bout those things
And I simply had to reply.

"Well, now I guess it'd be Christmas
With the little ones around to enjoy
All the grandeur of Santy and Poppy
And, yes, a toy and a toy and a toy."

But, I reminisced with a look back
To the good times when I was a teen
And said back then it'd have to be
HALLOWEEN!!!!

Ya' see, in a small town like where I grew up
There wasn't just a whole lot to do and see.
So you looked for fun and excitement
Where you could make it and find it easily.

So, come the end of October
When the spooks and goblins came 'round
We'd have lots of fun and excitement
In and around our little town!

Outhouses were there to be toppled
And windows were there to be soaped
We hollered, "Trick or Treat."
But it was really tricks for which we hoped.

Old Sam Cathy was our night watchman
But on Halloween night, he was our spy.
Down on one end of Main Street,
He'd warn us if someone were coming by.

Anybody foolish enough to leave
A car parked on a street downtown.
Could expect to find it next morning on a Coke case
Where the wheels would just spin round and round.

I guess you could call our fun
Pretty mundane and not really wild
But, it left us with a lot of good mem'ries
Growing up, on Halloween, in Whitney, as a child.

THE DEPOT

The Houston and Texas Central Railroad
came through Hill County in 1876
and fostered a town called Whitney
way out yonder in the Crosstimbers sticks.

Thence, the town I later called home
began to flourish and gradually grow.
And right smack in the middle of town
sat a beautiful, yellow, wonderful depot.

I remember that old depot as open and big.
A water tank stood near to the front door.
It seems that I also recollect a cinder bin.
And, inside, I remember the oiled pine floor.

That depot gave us a sense of connection
to the outside world we hardly knew.
For somewhere down those long rails
there was, for us, a world wide and new.

'cause, you see, when you grow up in a small town
you lived a life caught 'tween town and rails.
Biding our time, preparing ourselves
for life "out there" where we'd spread our sails.

Some of us spread our sails
Far from the town of our youthful times
While others preferred to stay close,
Choosing to avoid more stressful climes.

29

Whither we went,
Whether near or far away
We carried Whitney with us
It made us who we are today.

The things that give a place its sense of itself
include its churches, school, and picture show.
We were lucky in Whitney,
'cause we also had our Depot.

For those of you who grew up in the city,
this kind of fascination is strange
But, you're used to a dynamic life
We hardly ever saw real change.

Yes, the depot is a dying breed
It long ago bid Whitney goodbye
Just like the days of our youth
And the railroad track it stood nearby.

THE SOPHOMORE POET

"Where'd you get your love of poetry?"
someone asked the other day.
As I thought about it a little while,
there was only one thing to say:

"I'm not too sure, but I have a feeling
that it started back a long time ago
probably in Mrs. Epps English class
studying Chaucer, Longfellow and Poe."

As I thought further about those days,
those classes seemed never to end.
Memorizing poems, reciting them out loud;
Mrs. Epps reminding us, "Poetry is your friend."

As I've gotten older, my eyes weaken
my memory, once good, now pales.
But I'm sure as long as I live, I'll always remember
the Prologue to Chaucer's "Canterbury Tales":
> *Whan that Aprill, with his shoures soote*
> *The droghte of March hath perced to the roote*
> *And bathed every veyne in swich licour*
> *Of which vertu engendered is the flour*

On and on it went, splendid Olde English
We, reciting in Texas English, so clipped.
Looking back, I'm guessing ole' Geoff
Musta' been rollin' over in his Westminster crypt.

Memorization and recitation wasn't the only
"odiferous" experience we had in English II.
We also had to pen our own original odic lines—
minimum of eight lines, two verses, recited on the date due.

We wracked our brains, searching high and low
for all we had for rhyming words and phrases
that would satisfy, even edify, Mrs. Epps
and, just maybe pass and win her praises.

My day came and up to the front I went,
poem in hand, full of angst and dread.
Nervously, I hitched my britches, looked at my shoes,
cleared my throat, looked right at Mrs. Epps, and said:

GREED
Greed is an enemy that's eternal
You find it wherever you may
You find it in the people you know
And the people you see each day.

You find it in the big cities
And in the small villages, too
And if you don't watch what you're doing
It will be right here in you.

The class didn't erupt in laughter;
nor did they burst out in derision.
I watched Mrs. Epps for her response;
anxiously awaiting her critical decision.

Honestly, I don't remember what she said;
nor do I remember the grade she gave.
I only remember being hooked on this stuff;
a form of expression I'd take to the grave.

She must have liked my poem, I guess.
She sent mine and some more off someplace.
They ended up getting printed in some book.
It was bound in red and had "Young America Sings"
on its face.

It wasn't much of a book
Just something for parents to buy.
But, it made me feel 10 feet tall
And gave me incentive to try

My hand at writing more poetry
finding ways to make lines rhyme.
Now, in retirement, it's something
to do to fill up my time.

Mrs. Epps is gone now; so are the days
when we rhymed merely for the score.
But she started something that's outlived
the exercises I dreaded as a high school sophomore.

On August 23, 2008, my wife, Rita, and I celebrated our 50th wedding anniversary. For that occasion, I wrote the poem that follows. I included it in this volume, not so much that it reflects on country life, but that it summarizes, poetically, the lives of two "country kids" who've "come a long way" together. The title is taken from a recent song made popular by country singer, Alan Jackson.

REMEMBER WHEN…

Remember when we first met
I don't know, but I'll just bet
You probably thought I was a slob
Country as dirt, rough as a cob.
…remember when…

Big hat, tee shirt, long-legged jeans
Too cool for school; you know what I mean.
You were prim and proper, cute as a bug
I smiled at you, you responded with a shrug.
…remember when…

We were in Dolly Marie's class
I decided to make my pass
I asked you out, you said yes
Where it would end, we couldn't guess.
…remember when…

We dated that summer—what a blast!
We had no way of knowing if it would last.
That was a summer school I would long remember
I just couldn't wait 'til next September.
…remember when…

Well, that next school year just fairly flew
Before it was over, we both knew
That we wanted to be together for life
And, in the spring, you agreed to be my wife.
…remember when…

The time barely drug to August twenty-three
That's when our wedding was scheduled to be.
The knot was tied midst cheers and ovation
Then, off we sped for our home in College Station.

No Niagara Falls, no Riviera, no honeymoon at all
'cause A&M classes were beginning in the Fall.
What a first year of marriage. Our house was so small
You could stand in one corner and see it all.
…remember when…

You were wonderful as new-wed Aggie wife
Starching fatigues in the bathtub the first time in your life
You never really complained, though I sure would
You just starched and ironed the best you could.
…remember when…

In Aggie Wives Club you and Marilyn learned bridge
Taught Jerral and me and thought you had the edge.
But, we've beaten y'all badly all through the years
Y'all were better teachers than players, it's clear.

I do remember one spring evening on TV
The Academy Awards were on and y'all just had to see
So, up on the roof, Jerral and I grudgingly went
Put up the antenna, although the pole was bent.

Show watched, it was getting really late
Storm coming up, taking it down just couldn't wait
Back up on the roof we went grumbling all the way
Put it up again to see something else? THAT'LL BE THE DAY!
…remember when…

That senior year, we rented a much bigger place
Lots more room, a place to study, so much more space
The problem: it was across the street from a drive-in
Where every night, louder than thunder, Roy bellered "Cryin'"

The Army called, off to Benning we went
Nearly two years later, Little Craig was sent
To be nurtured spoiled, to be our joy.
First grandchild on both sides—what a spoiled little boy.

Army over, off we go to San Antone
A year and a half later, Craig wasn't alone
Here came Keith, a precocious little tyke
Cute as a bug, impossible not to like.

Our lives unfolded; off to Mississippi I took the three
Determined to try my best to get the PhD.
Long story short, with Rita's help, I did
While we were there Kevin became our third kid.

Our boys have brought so much joy to our lives
But, never more than the ladies they found to be their wives
Cheryl and Kerri are wonderful—in fact
You're places in the will remain—at least for now—intact!

To top it off, the best thing they ever did
Was present us with the most wonderful set of grandkids
Allie, Jason, Cadence, and Caroline—what a super crew
Nanny and Poppy are proud of each and every one of you.

We just pray that we can live long enough to see
Each of you grow and become the best you can be.
It matters less what you end up doing for a living
What matters most is that you do less taking than giving.

Our life's played out, much like a wonderful song
A poem including it all would be entirely too long.
I'll just hit a few highlights to finish this little ode
Of a few of the goods and bads along the road.

Sicknesses and accidents, we've sure had our share
Cancer, operations, car wrecks—but never more'n we could bear.
Through it all, so far, our faith's seen us through
Many would have been hard to take but not for you.

But, with all that, we've had a bunch of good times
Going to where cowboys make words rhyme
Traveling with our family and many good friends
Seeing what's just ahead beyond where the road bends.

Like skiing trips to Colorado with the family
And hearing that Keith went over a cliff smack into a tree.
Poppy going down a bunny slope all on his own
Ending up falling and breaking an anklebone.

We've seen all fifty states, lots of Canada, and Spain
'course I saw some of Scotland—some of it through pain
We've gone on cruises, driven thousands of miles
Remembering through many picture books brings many smiles.

You've suffered countless hours listening to my rhymes
I suspect, although I didn't see, through gritted teeth sometimes
Through it all, you've always given me good critiques
It's helped a lot with what might be called my poetic technique.

I guess when it's all said and done we've had a wonderful life
I've been blessed for the last 50 years having you as my wife.
Whatever years we have left together, maybe then
We can look back on these years and **Remember When**.

J.T. PELHAM
(1904-1971)

My dad, John Thomas (J.T.) Pelham was born in Tatum, Texas in 1904 and spent most of his early life outside the small community of Huron, north of Whitney. It is that time in his life, and some years thereafter, on which this series of glimpses into his life will focus. I wish I knew more about his life back then, but he was not the kind of man who talked much about his early life and I didn't know, when he was alive, that I would ever want to know a lot about it. Now, I wish I had asked. Nevertheless, I remember some of the stories he told about himself, and some I heard from others.

EDUCATION. Dad was a devout believer in the value of education. I can't remember there ever being any doubt that I would attend college after high school. Where did that kind of philosophy come from? Certainly, it didn't come from his parents or siblings. As far as I know, he was the only member of his family (three brothers and a sister) who ever went beyond the fifth or sixth grade. The little country school out in Huron didn't go much farther than that and there was little incentive in the family to stay through what was offered there, let alone going all the way into Whitney to matriculate in the "big school" down there (all of 10 miles or so). Of course, that was before there were buses to deliver students to town school and there certainly wasn't family transportation available for the trip. If one desired more schooling, and was so inclined, it was to be gained on one's own.

Dad, in his own "bullheaded" style, left home after completion of the schooling at Huron and moved to Whitney to continue his public school education. Can you imagine, in this day and time, a 14 or 15 year-old leaving home, moving into town on his own, making his own living—just to go to school? Neither can I, but off he went. When he got there, he had to have a job and a place to stay. He accomplished both by going to work in the kitchen of a local boarding house. I simply can't imagine what life must have been like for him. Working morning, noon and night in the boarding house, going to school, studying—there wasn't much time for a kid his age to get into trouble. Knowing him, I doubt that was a problem anyway.

The only thing I know about that experience was what I learned early in my life when I noticed a bad scar on his left (I think) leg, from the knee down to his ankle. It was the kind of scar that was bad enough that you could only imagine how much of his leg had been lost in the fire that caused it. The story I heard was that he was working in the kitchen late one night and the kerosene stove caught fire. As the fire raged, the kerosene must have leaked out of its container and spilled on the floor, where it immediately caught fire. The flames must have been horrible! Anyway, the outcome was that much of the flesh on the back of his leg was lost and, I'm guessing, the rehabilitation from that must have been hard. Needless to say, though, it didn't burn away his desire for more education.

After high school, he did what few people in his day did—he enrolled in Hill College, the county-supported junior college in the county seat town, Hillsboro. That would have been in approximately 1921 or 1922 and times were bad. As a result, the county couldn't support the school and it closed. Dad didn't let that put a halt to his quest for higher education and transferred to the junior college over in Meridian. There, the same thing happened! The school closed and, as the story goes, he went down the road to Clifton, where the scenario was repeated. Three colleges in three years—all closed. Undaunted, he went down to Huntsville and got a year or so of coursework at Sam Houston Normal Institute. He soon returned to his home in Hill County to begin what he hoped would be his life's work—education.

Education in rural Texas in the 20's wasn't easy. My dad had already experienced some of its hard times and overcome many of its obstacles. When he had completed all the higher education he was able to put together, he found just how difficult it could be for the practicing educator. His first job was in a "country school" in Hill County. How he got it provides an interesting glimpse into his tenacity and into the context of the educational system itself. The story goes that he went out to the school in question and found the farmer on whose land the schoolhouse was located. In those days the landowner also served as the "school board" and the person to whom an applicant must go seeking a teaching job. The old man was plowing and Dad went up to the fence and waited until he made the round back to the fence. Bringing the mules to a halt with an annoying, loud "WHOA," he asked Dad what he wanted. Hearing that he was applying for the open teaching position, he asked pointedly, "what kinda experience you got?" My Dad's only answer was, "none, sir," to which the old man replied that he wouldn't hire anybody without experience. My Dad got the job when he replied, "how do you expect me to get any experience if you won't hire me to teach in your school?" That completed the difficult preparation that he had gone through to get there and begin a career in teaching that lasted several years and covered several other "country schools" in central Texas.

One other episode that I heard from either my dad or from someone who "told" on him involved his teaching assignment in the Coon Creek School somewhere in the depths of the country in Bosque County. It inspired the following short poem:

It was Coon Creek School
In about nineteen twenty-five
My dad was teaching school
Just to keep himself alive.

Now, back in those days
Boys had little use for school or charm
They merely stayed in school
'til they were needed on the farm.

One day, some raw-boned boys
Challenged Dad to a fight
Maybe, they thought, we'll get in our bluff
Better yet, he'll run off in fright.

Well, it didn't turn out
Quite the way they'd drawn it up
After he'd whipped a couple of 'em
The biggest 'un ran off like a whipped pup!

LIFE AT HOME. If seeking an education and a career off the farm was difficult for a boy from the country in those days, life at home had to have been a mix of the bitter and sweet.

Bitter because life back then was hard. No electricity for the "necessities" we enjoy today; no running water for indoor usage; and difficult, backbreaking work under the worst of conditions to eek out a living for a large family on a small crop and livestock farm. While I don't recall my Dad talking much about those days, I know that's where he got his work ethic and his capacity to "make do" with little and "do the best with what he had." Interestingly, about the only things I remember him talking much about were some events that I'd classify as "sweet," or more fun times on the home place. A couple of them I'll share here.

It seems that he and one or more of his brothers were visiting with a couple of neighbor boys over the fence on the backside of their place one day. Daddy's brother had a 22 rifle that one of the neighbor boys really, really wanted, so they were talking trade. Whatever it was they decided on, the trade was consummated and the neighbor boy got his prize. As he stood admiring his newly gained hunting weapon, a terrible thing happened. Barefoot, as they always were during warm weather, the boy had rested the rifle on his foot—barrel down—and it went off! Shot a hole right through his foot! Clean as a whistle! Well, he had to do something so that his mother didn't get on to him and make him trade the offending weapon back, so he did the wisest thing he could think of. He went back home, soaked the foot in kerosene (the treatment of choice for wounds of that nature back then), put on socks, and wore shoes the rest of the summer.

In another episode, one of Dad's brothers was running barefoot (again) through a freshly picked cornfield. As he ran, he jammed a cornstalk into the bottom of his foot! Right up to the hilt! Well, he couldn't keep that from his mother very well, so he went home and came clean with what had happened. My grandmother dug out the shreds of the cornstalk as well as she could, applied ichthammol drawing ointment to it and applied a bandage. As might be expected, shards of cornstalk remained in the foot for months thereafter and my uncle couldn't wear shoes for months—even in the dead of winter!

I can just imagine the things those boys got into back then. So many boys, so close in age, and so far from town. It's no wonder they stayed so close throughout their adult lives. My dad and his younger brother carpentered together for a long time, including a stint at Fort Wolters Air Base near Wichita Falls. He was also close to his older brother and we visited them quite often when I was young. Closeness as young boys and men was manifest in later life and resulted in my being close in those days to my cousins.

One other image of my Dad's early life didn't occur as he grew up in the country, but as he lived in the country as a young man. It involves a problem with early automobile transportation, before the fuel pump was added to the internal combustion engine. That, coupled with the fact that most country roads were built where the "lay of the land" demanded. That is, there wasn't as much cutting of hills, thereby flattening out, or lowering the grades over which highways might run. That combination of carburetion by gravity flow and steep-graded hills caused many problems for the would-be automobile traveler. My Dad's experience with one such auto and one such hill inspired the following poem:

Back in the days
Of long, long ago
Auto engines were fed
By "gravity flow"

When the tank was full
And the car was running flat
Gas ran to the engine
And you got where you were going at.

But, if the tank wasn't full
Or you were going up a grade
The car might just stop
Then, my friend, I'm afraid

You might run back to where
You came from to here
In case you're on a steep hill
Your speed might pick up, I fear.

Out between Whitney and Blum
There's just such a hill
When going up forward, gas doesn't run,
Starving for gas, the engine it'll kill.

Those, like my Dad, who
Are good at making good out of worse
Just turns around at the base
And goes up the hill—IN REVERSE!

SAUCERED AND BLOWED

I don't reckon I ever saw my Dad
Drink coffee he didn't saucer and blow.
What's that? Some might very well ask.
Well, I'll tell those of you who don't know.

You see, fresh coffee's hot
Much too hot to drink or sip
'n if you ain't real careful
You'll burn your tongue and lip.

Daddy got up real early
He'd brew a pot and pour a cup
He'd pour a dab in the saucer
Blow on it; let it cool and then he'd sup.

I can remember him doin' that
Ever' mornin' before I went to the barn
To feed the sheep, milk the cow
And put out the hay, oats, and corn.

When he finished his coffee,
Off to the barn he'd go
Makin' sure I'd done what I should.
He was a demanding so-and-so!

After the chores were done
We'd go back to the house and eat
I don't remember a breakfast meal
Without eggs, biscuits, and some kind of meat.

Now, I never got the taste of coffee
It just didn't taste good at all
'course that all changed in the Army
Where the coffee was black and bitter as gall.

But, I never saucered and blowed it
That seemed to end with my Dad's generation
Now, that's just not *de rigueur*
It lacks a required level of sophistication.

One thing my Daddy wasn't,
Nor cared very much about
Was being considered sophisticated
He was what he was, without a doubt.

I've thought a lot about that habit
He had so many years ago
I don't know what's happened to it
But, there's one thing I do know.

We'd all be better off
If, over coffee, we took a lot more care
To saucer and blow, but it seems
Lingering over coffee is just time we can't spare.

Rather, we fill our travel mugs,
Drinking as down the road we drive
This has become a life metaphor
As faster and faster we strive.

Not stopping to smell the coffee
Let alone saucer and blow it
Life was slower and easier back then
Folks like my Dad seemed to know it.

There's been another use of the term
I've heard a lot thrown around
It refers to an act of ending something
A finishing, a conclusion, like a closing down.

Hence, someone will say, "Well,
we've got this 'un saucered and blowed"
Meaning it's over and done
Time to move down the road.

I guess, in that regard,
My Dad's finished carrying his load.
He's finished his coffee and his chores
And his life has, indeed, been **saucered and blowed.**

DADDY'S BOOTJACK

Over in the corner of our bedroom
There's an important part of my history.
Made of wood, not pretty or expensive
But, very important and meaningful to me.

It's just an old cyprus bootjack
Not something to write home about
Not very useful to most anyone else
Something most homes do well without.

But, to me, an important part
Of who I am and whence I came
A source of pride of my rural roots
And the worth of my Daddy's name.

You see, Daddy wore boots a lot
Sometimes they fit just a little too tight
He needed help to get them off
And the old jack did the job just right.

I'll describe what a bootjack is
For those of you who don't know
You see, it's a wedge-shaped device
With a heel-shaped notch to fit a boot just so.

You just step up on the jack
And slip your heel in the notch.
Pull up briskly, off comes the boot
No one has to help you; they just watch.

Just as I watched my Dad
So many years ago as a youth
Thinking, some day I'll do the same
Getting out of my boots.

So, now I use it, just like him
Makes me nostalgic when I do.
Don't know who'll get it
After I get through.

None of my sons wear boots
That'll end with my generation
I just hope Daddy's bootjack
Doesn't end up as a charity donation.

'cause it needs to be in a family
with ties back to my Dad.
Thinkin' it might go somewhere
Sure does make me kinda sad.

If it does go somewhere else
I hope a family member'll get it back.
It just don't seem right for someone else
usin' my Daddy's bootjack.

CONVERSATIONS IN A SMALL-TOWN DOCTOR'S WAITING ROOM

"When're they gonna call me,
I've been here nearly two hours.
Why so many with the same appointment time?
Tell me again, when's ours?"

I'm listening in to a conversation
Going on between two older men.
Waiting as patiently as I can for my appointment
And see if the doctor is really in.

"I remember when we'as kids," one continues,
"we didn't have all these new-fangled toys.
We played down on the creeks and fields;
Just me and a couple'a neighbor boys."

"Well," says his conversation mate
"we didn't have much time to play
seein' as how we had cows to milk, hay to haul
there wadn't a lot of time left at the end of our day."

"You know, the only fights me 'n my older bud
got into back in those days now long gone
wuz when we'd be milkin' and one or the other'd
squirt the other and the milkfight would be on."

Answered his friend, "Kids these days
don't know how to have that kind' a fun.
They've gotta have cars and gadgets,
and money to make the car run.

"I'd hoped one of my kids or grandkids
would' a took over one of the places I own.
You know, not a one of 'em did. In fact,
I've sold 'em all and moved into town."

That said, the conversation turned again,
this time, to the topic of gas well drilling.
Says one, "they ain't drilled on my place yet,
But, I'm shore more'n willing."

"Looks like to me, they's drilling all 'round me
I guess on them folks with lots a money
I know they just drilled on the place down the road.
That ole' boy's got more money than Burleson's got honey!"

As the crowd ebbed and flowed;
some going in, others coming out,
our conversationalists continued their musings
and that's how this poem came about.

I don't think you can find these kinds of discussions
taking place just every place at any time.
You really need to find yourself in a small town doctor's office
with waiting patients in chairs, against the wall, all in a line.

The following stories are a sampling of those told by my Mother-in-law, Norene Gage Letbetter. Mrs. Letbetter was born and raised in San Saba County, Texas and lived there, with short exceptions, all her life. In addition to my wife, Rita, she and her husband, Clovis, raised three sons. She's been active in her church all her life and still loves to play Scrabble, 42, and almost any other game—very well, I might add. These stories are summarizations of several hours of taped interviews with her and are examples of those she's told to her delighted grandchildren for many, many years.

DOLLY NORENE LETBETTER (1907-)

On Medicine Shows: "they'd come to town and didn't cost anything to go to 'em. They'd play some music and sing some songs and then they'd want to sell us some medicine. We never did buy medicine or anything, but they always sold candy that had prizes in it. We didn't have enough money to buy candy, but I always watched others get it and I wanted some. The prizes were little dolls and maybe scarves...they didn't amount to anything. The entertainment mainly was jokes and music. Sometimes they'd dance. They'd be set up on trailers with a tarp on it with bales of cotton to sit on."

On where they lived: "We lived south of San Saba on what we called the Burns Place. We had to walk to town, to school, to the skating rink, about two-and a half miles. There were lots of rattlesnakes. It's a wonder we didn't' get bit.

We didn't have electricity on our place and we had a milk cooler made out of tin. Momma would use a cloth device and would run water down through it somehow to keep the milk and butter cool. If a cloth covering the milk would blow off, dirt would get in it. We'd just let it settle to the bottom (for my take on that, see "Milking")"

For heating, we had a fireplace and we'd have to bring in wood to burn in it. We'd get cold because we didn't have glass in the windowpanes. We had kerosene lamps. We didn't get rural electricity until around 1941. We finally got a kerosene refrigerator after Rita (oldest child) was born. That was about the time we got our first Aladdin lamp."

On personal grooming: "I always wanted to look pretty. I rolled my hair up on corn shucks. I'd go to the corncrib and get shucks and put 'em in water so I could tie them in knots. I'd roll my hair up in them and tie them up. When I unrolled it, my hair would frizz up all over the place. I always thought that was really pretty. There were nine of us kids and we couldn't keep combs. Daddy would buy us one and somebody would lose it. So we'd go to the kitchen and get us a fork and use that to comb our hair. There were five of us girls and four boys. We didn't have hair spray, but it was stylish to use Bryllantine. It was greasy, but we thought it was kind of pretty."

On dating: "They were having the July Jubilee over at Brady and Clovis came over to get me to go to it. We didn't have any screens on our windows and we had an old hen that always came into the house to lay her eggs. Just as he drove up, the old hen flew out the window. It really did embarrass me and I figured he'd never come back to see me…but he did and later we got married."

On hard work: "We had to work real hard. We were awfully poor. Us kids would have to help Daddy pick cotton at our place and when we were through there, we'd pick cotton for other people. We had to do that to buy our school clothes. We never did get to start school when the new year began, because we were still picking cotton when school started. We also had to pick up pecans. We worked in the field just like the boys did.
Us girls had to clean the house, fix the meals, and wash the clothes. When we washed the white clothes, we had to boil them and add bluing

to the water. We used lye soap that we made every time we killed a hog.

Speaking of killing a hog, we did that every year during the winter. Daddy'd put the carcass in scalding water to get the hair off them. We made lye soap and cracklin's out of the skin.

I was real fast picking up pecans. I liked that better than picking cotton, but we did that, too."

On school: "We had to walk to school. It seems we used to have colder winters back then and it was awfully cold walking to and from school—seems we walked into the north wind both ways. The water fountain was on the outside and icicles would form around the fountain. After I'd come in, my hands were so cold; they'd hurt when they thawed out. I wanted to cry but I didn't because I was afraid the teacher would whip me."

On entertainment: "We'd go to dances after I got older. We had a fair every summer in August, so we'd go to that. They'd have hobbyhorses and ferris wheels. Daddy would always buy our school shoes in August. I'd always get mine too little and wear them to the fair. My heels would be blistered by the time we got through. (Why did you get them too little?)…I didn't know they came in different sizes, so if they looked pretty, I'd take them. I don't know why the man who sold them to us wouldn't tell us that they came in different sizes.

We had a picture show in town and Wilma (sister) and I liked to go to the Wednesday matinee. Lots of times, Momma wouldn't have a dime to give us to get in, so we'd take eggs to sell so we could go. Lots of those eggs would be soft-shelled so I'd take them the first part of the 2-½ mile trip and I'd make Wilma carry them the last part, so if they started to break, it'd be on her. The first show I saw was at the fair. It was a silent one, with captions on the bottom of the screen.

I never did have a pretty doll. I had one that was stuffed with sawdust. My sister got one after she got big enough to pick cotton and made enough money to buy her a baby doll. We'd cut paper dolls and pictures of furniture out of the catalogue and play with them."

On milking: "We ran a dairy and anytime I wanted to look good, the old cow would have cockleburs in her tail and she'd switch it around and scratch my face, or get her tail tangled up in my hair… I had a hard time looking pretty."

On our first radio: "We were too poor to buy a battery, so Daddy would take the battery out of the truck so we could listen to it. The speaker sat on top of the radio. It was real pretty… it looked like a ship. We had a neighbor who didn't have a radio, so she'd call us up on the telephone and want us to hold the phone up to the speaker so she could listen to the radio. We would do it for her. San Saba didn't have a radio station, so about the only station we could get was WBAP out of Fort Worth (approximately 150 miles away)."

On education: "We only had 11 grades in school and I only went about half way through the ninth grade. None of my four brothers or four sisters graduated from high school. It was not uncommon for kids to drop out of school in those days. My best friend dropped out of school before I did so I was not happy after that. The main reason I dropped out was that I had to help my older sister take care of her 16-month-old child who had the measles. I got so far behind that I couldn't catch up. I promised my folks I'd go back, but I never did."

On caring for the elderly: "We liked to go to town on Saturday nights, where people would buy their groceries and sit in their cars and visit with each other. Well, one time we wanted to go to town, but Granny was staying with us. She was bedfast and Momma said we couldn't go off to town and leave her there. We solved that by putting a mattress in the back of the pickup and hauling her to town with us."

On San Saba: "The streets of San Saba weren't paved. An old man had a horse-drawn sprinkler wagon and he would go along the streets and spray water on them to hold down the dust."

On Aunt "Rildy": "She was my favorite aunt. She never did get married. She liked to make lemon chess pies and us kids always liked to eat them. She'd bring her guitar and sing to us. Some of the songs she'd sing were silly and some were real sad. Two of the silly songs she sang went like this:

"Oh, they make rat pies over there, over there
they make rat pies over there,
They make rat pies and flavor them with flies
And they'll kill you if you eat 'em over there."

"There was a little pig who lived on a farm
the crazy little thing did lots of harm
uh, uh, uh, uh
There was a little pig who lived on a farm
The crazy little thing did lots of harm
uh, uh, uh, uh
The rest of this song lays on the shelf
if you want to sing it, you can sing it yourself
uh, uh, uh, uh"

The next three poems are written about, and dedicated to, three of the greatest guys I know—my sons. Most fathers can understand and agree with my pride in the accomplishments of their sons. Whatever we were and whatever we did, we bring with us as we raise our sons, see them grow to adulthood, achieve their educations, pursue their careers, marry or not, raise families or not, and become men. I'm duly proud of my sons and the lives they are living. Thanks, guys.

CRAIG

First sons are special
In their own unique way
We were thrilled when you came
And still are today.

You've been a real joy
A gem of great wealth
We've been so proud of you
Through all your sickness and health.

I'll never forget that fourteenth day of April
Ninety hundred and sixty-two
Fort Benning's Martin Army Hospital
We were so proud to finally have you!

You didn't know it at the time
But I wasn't there to witness your arrival
I was flying back from Fort Stewart
In a little puddle-jumper, praying for my survival!

You were the first grandchild on both sides
And, you just happened to be cute as a pup.
No matter where we went and who we saw
They just always wanted to eat you up!

Our world turned upside down
Not long after we got to College Station
You got terribly sick, was hospitalized;
We were deep in our desperation.

But, you and we came through it
You were a fighter through it all
Through it, you learned a valuable lesson:
"Always find a way to get up no matter how bad the fall."

Your school years were another source of pride
Not only smart, you were good with your hands, too
Always made good grades in most everything
Could fix radios and electronics to work like new.

Didn't take long to see where you were headed
To Aggieland to make your educational way
So good in computer science
But, got your degree in something called BANA.

One of the things for which I was most proud
Was your time spent in the co-op plan
Working nights out at TMPA
Preparing yourself to be a workingman.

Since your graduation, you've really excelled
Always had good jobs, with responsibility
From Eddie Chiles to Neiman-Marcus
You were successful because of your ability.

I can't finish this commentary on your ability
Without thanking you for all your help
With me and our friends and our computers
I certainly could never do any of it by myself.

Somehow, you've done all this
And maintained a love of music and song
Your skill with a guitar is a mystery to me
And has been all along!

For all your success and ability
The best thing you've done or did
Was marrying a girl named Cheryl
And giving us our wonderful grandkids!

We're so proud of you and all of you
We just can't brag enough.about 'em
From Ally's dancing to Jay's baseball
We don't what we'd do without 'em.

The Gaelic word, "crag" is the origin of your name
It stands for enduring, steadfast, and strong
These words describe you better than can I
And, we've known they did all along.

KEITH

*"emotional, kind, sensitive, intelligent, smart, always
exceptionally well-presented yet charmingly down-to-earth.
wacky sense of humor"*

Those words are said to describe "Keith"
And do so for our Keith no doubt.
Anyone who knows him or has met him
Know they tell us what he's all about.

Born on January twenty-fifth,
nineteen sixty-five in the city of San Antone
Independent from day one
He certainly had a mind of his own.

Sucked his thumb, the Doc said OK
"He'll stop in his own time."
He did, but not by our hand
He made up his own mind.

What a guy, athletic to his core
Went through the house just a' reeling
Running and jumping
Always trying to touch the ceiling.

Always jumping, he played church ball
Wasn't supposed to dunk, but just the same
He did one night, to his delight
But had to sit out the next game.

I've always thought he was at least
One of the best young fielders I ever saw
I could hit ground balls to him forever
Asked him if he wanted to quit, he'd say, "Naw."

He'd wear out the back of his glove
Keeping it low on the ground
Good with the bat and glove
In fact, pretty good player all around.

He wasn't bad at football
But baseball was his best game
Could have played college ball, I'm sure
But senior year, mono called his name.

After you graduated high school
We moved to Missouri and left him on his own
Our only contact with him for months
Was by way of telephone

So, we didn't really know
How sick you really were
Finally, it dawned on us
We needed you up there.

You began to get better
And went on back
Then, in college,
You began to get on track.

Since college graduation
You've really come into your own
You've become the confident young man
We've always known.

Yes, as the descriptors said above
They fit you very well: intelligent, smart,
well-presented yet charmingly down-to-earth.
Plus, you've got lots and lots of heart.

You've really found your calling
Your success is due to your intelligence and charm
We're so very proud of you and trust that you
Will continue to be hard working, trustworthy, and warm.

KEVIN

Not knowing, but pretty sure
It's tough being the third boy
Having to wear all THEIR clothes
And playing with THEIR toys.

As our third, and last, son
That was Kevin's long, sad plight
He had to live up to their names
And he had to learn how to fight.

To add to his "last son plight"
Another problem befell as soon as he landed
He came into life, like his Dad
With the curse of being left-handed.

Of course, that curse was a blessing
When he started baseball at about age eight
We found, at that tender age,
That he could throw the baseball hard and straight.

That trait gave us many pleasant nights
Coaching and watching many, many games
Had a really good left-handed curve ball
But, you just had to remind him where to aim.

Went with us to Columbia and ole Mizzou
Played baseball there from the time we landed
There I saw the strangest sight ever on a diamond
The entire 13-year-old infield was LEFT-HANDED.

Played high school ball for the Kewpies
Played summer baseball, too
Even went to the Babe Ruth World Series
Playing on All-Star teams all the way through.

Following your last year in summer ball
Your Mom and I had withdrawal pains
We'd been going to games for seventeen years
Didn't now what to do on Summer nights again.

After a college career that, at times,
Was just a little "iffy"
You followed us to Texas
And got a job in a jiffy.

Since that time you've
Never been unemployed
For more than a few days
And we've always enjoyed

Seeing how you can go
From job to job, with hardly a pause
;I've never known how you do it
but, I guess it's just because

of your wonderful personality.
You obviously interview well.
You come across as a born salesman
A trait any hirer can always tell.

Your life, today,
Is so much more serene
And it's largely due to
Kerri's arrival on the scene.

And it's not only her
But two beautiful daughters, too.
We love K.K. and Caroline so
And for that we thank the two of you.

The Gaelic words for Kevin
Includes the adjectives "gentle" and "kind"
Anyone who really knows you well
Agree that's what your name brings to mind.

MELIA AZEDARACH

Most country homes
Had at least one in the yard
The limbs were twisted
The berries rock hard.

Not much to look at
In fact, not pretty at all
Needed so much water
Soaked up what rain would fall.

A deciduous tree
Of the mahogany strain
Native of China and India
At home also on the Fertile Plain

How they got to our shores
Nobody really seems to know
Brought over for their timber
They found our soil perfect to grow.

Too perfect, it would seem
In fact, they've sprung up everywhere
Look out almost any back farm door
It's pretty likely you'll see one there.

When the beries get ripe and fall
They make a terrible, gooey, mess
When tracked in through the backdoor
The goo gave my Mom no small distess.

But to those of us too young to care 'bout that
The berries provided, not mess, but ammo
Load one in a slingshot, aim it at your foe
And let go that missile, WHAMO!!

Those berries, when nice and green,
Will make a whelp wherever they hit
I guarantee you when you're hit by one
It's a feeling you won't soon forget.

They say one man's poison
Is another man's meat
So, although Mom didn't like those things
For us boys, they were pretty neat.

'cause when you're young on the farm
You kinda make fun where you find it
And, if Mom doesn't like what you're doing
You can always say, "So and so was behind it."

Not that would always buy you
Any kind of long-term dispensation
Mom had a way of saving things up
'til you messed up on another occasion.

I guess I should identify the plant
That was the source of lots of trouble for me
Its scientific name, *MELIA AZEDARACH*,
Is better known to us as the lowly Chinaberry Tree.

The Chinaberry, not quite as hated
As it's neighbor, the dreaded mesquite,
But, in many ways similar in nature
Beautiful only to the most aesthete.

So, consider the Chinaberry Tree
Berries for fun, timber from the trunk
Berries, toxic, if ingested by humans,
But, for birds, a way of getting really drunk!

HORSELESS COWBOYS

Think all cowboys ride horses
Dress in kerchiefs, chaps and such,
Live in line camps half their lives
And don't go into town all that much?

Well, I know guys who work the land
Who run cattle right along with the best
Who don't ever chase cows astride a horse
But, whose "cowsense" will stand most any test.

While visiting my brother-in-law recently
I was privileged to ride on his coattails.
He had just bought some good black baldies
At a special San Saba cow sale.

He had 'em penned in a patch by the barn
Getting used to their home, allaying their fears.
Before turning them out in a bigger pasture
He needed to put ID tags in their ears.

Bein' an old hand, I went along
Thinkin' I can help him, no doubt
Although used to working alone,
He tolerated me helping him out.

Regarding attire, I must tell you
He wore neither kerchief nor chaps.
Rather, his work attire consisted of
Worn jeans, tough brogans and a battered baseball cap.

There was no hoopin' and hollerin'
Rather, he spoke to them softly and clear.
Gently urging them to follow,
Saying, "sook" and "come on here."

Despite his coaxing and pleading
There was one old black muley, of course
Who wouldn't come and him on foot
'cause he doesn't even own a horse.

About then, I heard the sound of a tractor
And him, on it, going after her.
Astride a John Deere 2355 cutting horse.
I thought I'd die of laughter.

Well, she started towards the barn
With him nippin' on her tail.
When she went right, so did he
Left, the same, without fail.

When he penned her, I had to comment,
"That tractor'll plow a field, dig postholes and such.
In fact it's so much better'n a cutting horse,
and it didn't cost or eat nearly as much."

The epilogue to this little story
I'll say surprised me no end.
He told me that four-wheelers
Are used by many of his ranching friends.

"Four-wheelers replacing horses?!,"
said I, in wild disbelief.
"It's mostly used," he said,
"for the horses' relief."

Two reasons, he explained
For this unexpected change.
One, it's easier on the horses
Two, they work well on wild range.

So, just because he don't dress like a cowpoke
Or ride his horse when he works his herds.
Don't go thinkin' he's no cowboy
'cause he might just have you eatin' yore word.

....

Well, I thought I'd seen it all
When it comes to cow wranglin' by machine
'til a couple a days ago playin' golf
I'd come to the eighth green.

There, just off to the left of the green
Stood this little black Brangus bull
Just munching on the lush grass
Getting' his pore old belly full.

His foray into this bountiful repast
Was brought to an end on his owner's part
As he came down to drive him home
Herdin' him home ridin' a green golf cart!

STANDING IN LINE

Have you ever noticed;
Or is it just me, not you
The guy in the next line
Always gets through 'fore I do.

It always happens when I'm in line
People in front seem to be in slow motion.
I feel myself begin to get antsy,
Impatient, thinking I might succumb to the notion

Of screaming, "Get on with it,
I'm in a terrible hurry to check out"
What in the world are you doing;
What is this infernal holdup all about?

There he is, an "older gentleman"
Trying the self-check machine
Punching buttons, looking puzzled,
Muttering to himself, "What does all this mean?"

He finally gets everything out of his basket
Gets it checked and in the bag
Then, fumbling in his pocket and his wallet,
Now I'm wondering what's up with the snag.

Then, I see what's the problem
He can't figure out how to make payment
I fidget some more, clear my throat real loud
You could say I couldn't be less impatient.

Another instance in another store,
(and please pardon my sexist attitude,
after all, I just finished a diatribe
about that "older gentleman" dude)
there's this little lady woman
who's just putting her stuff on the belt.
Carefully, she places them one by one
Never to finish, I'm sure I felt.

Needless to say, she finally got through
Then, I really began to feel put upon
Carefully, to my insensitive disdain
She starts pulling out thousands of **COUPONS**!

Those dastardly coupons
Each one worth such and such discount
As she, in slow motion, scans each one
My hostility, now nearing homicidal, continues to mount!

I check my watch; I shuffle my feet
I cough 'til my throat's quite raw
She continues to scan coupons
I'm sure she's the slowest human I ever saw.

Well, she finally finished with the coupons
I thought I'd surely seen the worst
WRONG! How wrong I was
'cause now she's just opening up her purse.

Digging, diving, shuffling stuff side to side
Muttering to herself, "where can it be?
I know my checkbook's in here somewhere.
When did I use it last...let's see...

73

I remember now, it was in the clothing store
I wonder if I left it there."
"I'm sorry, sir, I seem to have lost my checks
Are you in a hurry to go somewhere?"

"No," says I. "My meeting's long over
and I'm sure my wife's surgery went just fine.
I've enjoyed spending the last quarter of my life
WAITING HERE, BEHIND YOU, STANDING IN LINE!!

GOD'S NEWEST TENOR

God's got a new tenor
Up there in his heavenly band
Says he's the best he's ever had
And the voice is just as good as the man.

Those of us who know him
Will agree with just what he says
He's the same up there as here
He sure hasn't changed any of his ways.

No, Ron's the same up there
As he was when he was here on Earth
A friend to be treasured
Indeed, "a pearl of great worth."

Friendly, trustworthy
Honest as the day is long
But the thing that made him special
Was what he could do with a song.

Man, could that guy sing
Got the most out of every song.
I cherished the times when I could sing by him
By him, very few of my notes went wrong.

I recall the first time we went
To the Lakeside 4th Thursday concert
He said, "Find a song or two to lead"
"I've never led singing" was all I could blurt.

"Not only that," he continued
"You're singing with a quartet."
"Never sung with a quartet," says I.
Says he, "well, not yet!"

Well, long story short, I did and we did
And I enjoyed it more than he knew
Made those 4th Thursday nights
Something we looked forward to.

Another "singing memory"
I have of Ron to share
Marcia and I sing with the Pecan Singers
And we finally got Ron there.

Oh, how I loved singing next to him
As we sung those old Christmas songs
He always knew just the right notes
And, somehow, I managed to sing along.

The last time I was privileged to sing with him
Was at the 4th of July celebration
What a day! We sang all those old standards
Honoring, as we do, the birth of our nation.

As much as I enjoyed his singing
I appreciated his love of cowboy rhymes
Seein' him smile at some of my stuff
Were some of my happiest times.

He was good at making others feel good
Could bring out the best in everyone
You'd bust your buttons to please him
And, he'd return it in kind when you were done.

Ron, every day we surely do miss you
As we fight our little daily fires
But, we know you're up there enjoying yourself
Singing first tenor in God's Holy Choir.

COWBOY CHURCH

Everywhere you go, it seems to be so
You see nestled in the woods
'neath a wooden cross, a rail to tie your hoss
A church preachin' the news that's Good.

Cowboy churches far and near, with voices clear
Are preachin' good news to all
Reachin' folks of the land, offerin' up a hand
'n, over and over, they're hearin' the call.

They're sweepin' the nation, a religious sensation
These churches deep in the wildwood
Throwin' down a rope, offerin' hope
To those who need to hear the news that's Good.

There's no fancy pulpit, but I submit
The cedar log one will do just fine
It's the message that's told that'll save yore soul
And keep yore steps in line.

You'll enjoy the songs, sing right along
They're old with old shape notes
I love it so, it's "get up and go"
You'll sing 'til you wear out yore throats.

These folk don't dress just to impress
It's cowboy boots, bonnets, and hats.
But, they're clean and neat from head to feet
They come but to worship and that's that.

If'n you're goin' for show, it's not here you oughta' go
These folks are here to praise the Lord
Their love for Him is sincere, that's why they're here
To sing, pray, and study the Word.

When God opens yore eyes, 'n you want'a be baptized
The baptistery's a galvanized stock tank
Don't matter what it's in, when God saves you from sin
Just get in, go under, and come up with Thanks.

So, if yore lookin' for a place that'll put a smile on yore face
And put you right up on the catbird's perch
Head on down to that place right outside'a town
And worship with us at the Cowboy Church.

PETE AND THE PREACHER

"Been thinkin' lots 'bout my soul,"
said Pete, the cowboy, the other day.
He was talking to the Reverend Cole
right after church on the Lord's Day.

"I don't rightly know 'bout how I fit;
seems ever'body else's more righteous'n me.
I ain't much to go to church, bein' blunt about it.
Seein's how I day-work way out on the Circle T."

"'sides that," he continues, much in the way of confession
"I don't hear much said in church 'bout people like me.
Seems preachers is always beggin' for faith professions
'n I ain't never been one to do that, don't you see."

"Facts is, I spend lots more'a my time outdoor
studying how our cattle is comin' along
than goin' to church reg'lar anymore.
I reckon by church standards, that's just plumb wrong."

"Well," says the Reverend Cole, "you might be surprised
to know that the Bible has more to say
about people like you and your work than you realized.
'cause, see, that's the way things were back in Biblical days."

The reverend's right, as you might expect.
Pete had lots of ancestors ahead of him.
God showed lots of love and respect
For all His creatures, 'cause He made all of them.

80

"Pete," Reverend Cole said after a brief delay
"we'll just take a stroll through the Good Book
'n see what all it has to say
'bout the subject. Let's take a look."

"Did you know, Pete, that some expert said
the Bible mentions the horse more'n a thousand times?
Why, when the Book of Revelation is read
The role of the horse comes through clear in those lines."

Pete's getting' into it now and says, "Yeah, that's true,
I 'member the story 'bout Jesus' birth long time ago
Some'a them folks who came to see 'im was like me'n you.
Them sheepherders came a long, long ways to show

how much they loved the new-born baby
'n brought him presents 'n honored him.
Preacher Cole, do you think maybe
I might be a little bit like them?"

"Yes, Pete," Reverend Cole agreed.
"I expect they were an awful lot like you.
See, they cared for their flocks and all their needs
Just like you care for your cattle and all your crew."

"You know sumpthin' else, Preacher Cole?
That story 'bout baby Jesus bein' born in a stable;
if'n you ain't never seed the beauty of a new-born foal
You might just think that whole story was just a fable."

"Pete, you're getting into it now, but
You need to know the Bible has a lot more to say
'bout the subject we've been talking about—
comparing our present conditions to yesterday.

See, the Good Lord's heart was just plumb filled
With His love for His creatures large and small
Psalms 50:10 says He owns all the cattle on a thousand hills
And He don't have any need for a bull from your stall.

What He's sayin' is that He's the boss of His outfit
He don't need anything from the likes of you 'n me
'cept that our love and adoration don't ever quit
and that we oughta live so that ever'body else can see

that we've been branded with His brand
'n that we're a part of His remuda and crew,
'n we oughta be in the saddle with reins in our hand
ridin' hard to share His word with people like me 'n you.

The bottom line, Pete, is He loves us
'n it's a love that's bigger than anybody else's
He expects us to love and honor Him, plus
He wants us to love others like we love ourselves.

When you think about it, that's pretty good advice
Whether you're talking about people or stock.
That's more'n just treatin' people nice,
It's doin' what's needed ever'day, 'round the clock."

"Whew," says Pete, with more'n a hint of surprise.
"I never thought of this whole thing that way.
Yore talk has shore 'nuff opened these ole eyes.
Maybe I'm not as far outta the loop as I thought 'fore today."

"I promise you're not, Pete. In fact, with a little help
we can have you right where the Lord wants you.
Right back sashayin' with Him step by step
Bein' a helpin' pard to them that don't know what to do."

"One last thing, Parson, they's one thing I know
The Bible says He'll come without no warnin'
I reckon we oughtta' do our chores 'n live our lives just so…
So, I reckon I'd best see you in church Sunday mornin'.

MEMORIES:
I'VE COME A LONG WAY, BABY

A good friend of mine and the mother of another good friend, Norma Slocum, wrote this poem. Gail Lorey, was born Jan 13, 1916, in a farming community in Knox County, Missouri, where she still resides. She was married and had three children. She says she has lived 93 years by running fast and not looking back!! She enjoys reading, crocheting, quilting, card games, and adores her grandchildren and great grandchildren. Her poetry reflects her life and that of her many friends. I selected this poem of hers because it reflects her early years in rural Northeast Missouri. Again, the reader is reminded of the similarities between her early experiences and those of others in this book—especially the way they embraced their lives and made the most out of what most moderns might look at with thoughts of "how could they live like that?"

Often times I stop to ponder
    As down "Memory Lane" I wander
When a lad named Levi Vansickle
    Married a gal named Etta Conder.

Started married life in a three room house
    Remembering makes me frown
It sat atop an old clay hill
    Seven miles from any town

They didn't have much money
    But were happy as could be
One year later had a baby boy
    And they named him Leonard Lee.

He ruled the roost the next four years
    He was their only baby
Then a little black-haired girl was born
    And Mother named her Sadie.

Then, two years later—I'll let you guess
    'cause this is quite a tale
Another little girl showed up
    Named Minerva Abigail.

Now, there were five "Vansickles"
    We were crowded as could be
But nine years later—room or not,
    Came baby Etta Marie.

Now there were six in that little house
    And it didn't have a bath
No running water, lights or heat
    Just three rooms and a "path."

But this house was "air conditioned"
    We "chinked" the windows and the door
On a windy day the old linoleum
    Would blow right up—off the floor!

An old wood heater kept us warm
    At least, it done its best
The lid was in three pieces
    It was broke—"like all the rest"!!!

Yeah! We did have running water
    Oh! That would make you cry
Someone had to run and pump it
    And hope the well would not run dry.

Let's not forget the "Thunder Mug"
    That "pot" caused many a fight.
Who would take it out each morning,
    And bring it in at night!

We all went to a "country school"
    Mt. Vernon was its name
You learned "Readin', Writin', and "rithmetic"—
    Or you had yourself to blame.

We learned to swim and dance and skate
    And in due time, allowed to date.
The boys came in—like a young man "oughter"
    No honkin' out front for Levi's daughter."

When winter came and the trees were bare
    We had to don "long underwear"
To keep out the cold it can't be beat
    But, oh, how I hated "that old drop seat"

But there was "Love" in that little house
    Enough to burst the seams
Dad thought to build a bigger house
    That always was his dream!

We've seen good times and bad times
    Of this, I don't jest
But we've always come through
    When put to the test!

We now drive a good car
    Automatic? You bet!
But that "old Model T"
    I will never forget!

We now push a button for lights
    Turn a faucet for water
If you don't appreciate that
    Then you surely had "oughter."

"Yep," times surely have changed
    Since I was a bride
Our old life style has passed
    And we can face it with pride!

We enjoy nice modern heat
    And rugs on the floors
Go to the bathroom inside
    And do the cookin' outdoors.

These "hard times" made us stronger
    It's behind us—"Well, maybe"
I'm gonna' lay back and enjoy it.
    I've come a Long Way, Baby."

Gail "Gooch" Lorey 1991

YOU THINK YOU'VE GOT PROBLEMS?

As I've gotten older
I've noticed some rather strange sensations
My eyes have grown weaker, my hair grayer
And my heart sometimes has some strange palpitations.

I don't want to attribute it to my increasing age
I was the same age, it seems, just a while ago.
I didn't feel then like I feel now
Somebody please tell me why that's so.

My income's down, my medicine bill's up
My memory's gone; my fingers tremble
Energy's down, fatigue's up
My feet and hands not nearly as nimble.

What is this that's got me all wrinkled?
What is this dreaded malaise?
What is this sorry state of affairs
That bothers me all of my "latter days"?

Well, somebody just wizened me up
Why my brain has shrunk and my feet have swollen
They pointed out the obvious:
What Mother Nature gave, Father Time has stolen!

TOO MUCH HUSBAND, TOO LITTLE MONEY

Think you've got it bad?
I'll tell you 'bout the life I've had
There's been more sad than glad
And, it's all because of a man
You've had it rough, too?
Well, let me tell you
Your misery can't hold a candle to
My life with dear old Stan.

Stan wasn't nothin' but a louse
Spent all his time 'round the house
He didn't do nothin' but grouse
Never brought home enough dough
To cover all the bills we owed
Mama said I should'a knowed
'bout the trap he'd throwed
But, I still walked into it though.

Try as hard as I might
I can't blame him for my plight
I've got all my hearing and sight.
No, I made the nest I'm livin' in
I sure did lose my head
Should'a heard what Momma said;
Well, I made this sorry bed
But, I'm sure not givin' in.

I should have seen the sign
I could'a found a better find.
But, I've made up my mind
I'm gonna ditch that sorry Stan
After all this time, I'm sure
Tired of bein' dirt poor
But, I know the cure:
This time, I'm gonna marry a RICH MAN!!!

SKEET'S MRI

Out fixin' fence the other day,
Skeet turned to Butch with this to say,
"Butch, I'm havin' a MRI in a coupla' days
so, you'll be workin' with Ira Hayes."

"What's a MRI? I never hearda' such,"
(course, Butch ain't been out much)
"Well," says Skeet "is a big-time 'zamination
they use to check out yore phys'cal contaminations."

"What's it mean, that MRI," asks Butch.
Cause, as 1 said above he never heard of such.
"Well," says Skeet, without hint of hesitation,
"It stands for Medicinal Relevancy Imagination."

"What's it 'sposed to do" Butch asks with expectancy.
Skeet says, "it's used for ever'thang from broke bones to pregnancy.
See, they shoot this little electrified mecruical ray
Right into yore body whilst on that table you lay."

"Why you gotta have it Skeet," into it now, Butch asks,
(thinking about assuming all the fence-building tasks)
"Well," says Skeet, "'member 'bout a month ago
when we's up to th' Baxter place in the drivin' snow?

"and 'member me runnin' straight under that oak saplin',
'n I hit my head, fell off my hoss, 'n couldn't recollect it happenin'.
Well, the sawbones says, after quite a lotta discussion,
from a hit like that you got what's called a repercussion."

"So, this Magical Resuscitation Imagination
will help to tell him if'n there's any brain inflammation.
I reckon brain inflammation ain't much of a good thing
'specially when you're punchin' cows, buildin' fences and everthing."

"Well," Butch says, with a hint of dread,
"what're they gonna do, cut off yore head?"
"Don't rightly know," is Skeet's reply.
"But they ain't gonna cut off my head, 'cause I might die."

"I 'spect as how they'll bandage it up a little,
'n in a coupla days, I'll be fit as a fiddle.
Least ways, I ain't 'bout to miss next week's rodeo
seein's how I gotta win some'a that go-round dough."

A few days pass, and the discussion recommences.
"Butch," says Skeet, "I ain't gonna be fixin' no more' a these fences."
"How come," asks Butch, seeing his future before his eyes.
Worried more about his sorry fate than if his friend Skeet dies.

"I cain't do it no more, my friend. The doc said so today;
He also said no more punchin' cattle 'n haulin' hay.
Says I got this bad place in my head that'll always give me pains.
Says that blow on my head must'a scrambled my brains."

"What're you gonna do, Skeet, I ain't never heard' a such."
(remember like I said before, Butch ain't been out much)
"How you gonna live, ifn you cain't do ranch work.
You ain't gonna be very good bein' a grocery store clerk."

Skeet retorts, "I ain't gonna clerk no grocer's store.
They's gotta be somethin' more
I can do without it hurtin' my brain.
Doin' bookwork and such'll drive me insane."

Puzzling and wondering where his life will lead,
Skeet turns to his friend, Miz Smith in his time of need.
Miz Smith, see, is the counselor at the local school
and surely she can help old Skeet retool.

"Miz Smith, what'm I gonna do with my life now;
all's I know to do is ridin' hosses and punchin' cows.
If'n you cain't help me, I don't rightly know who can.
Won't you just help me to make a plan?"

"Why, yes," was Miz Smith's helpful reply.
"We'll just talk a bit and together we'll try
to come up with something you can do
to turn your life around and start anew."

"Now, just exactly what did the doctor say
when you met with him the other day?"
"Says he," Skeet responds, not knowing where this was going,
"this thing is bad enough you could go without even knowing

what hit you. It could go just that fast.
And I just can't tell you how long this problem might last.
I don't mind tellin' you, Miz Smith, that scared me a lot
'n ain't much has scared me since I was a little tot."

"Interesting," Miz Smith said when Skeet finished his rambling.
"And you said he said something about your brain scrambling?"
"Yeah," said Skeet, "I didn't know 'zackly how that could be
seein's how I can still talk 'n walk 'n smell 'n see."

"What he meant," explained Miz Smith,
ready to proceed and none too soon
"was that the brain is encapsulated in the skull like a moth in a cocoon.
When the brain is bothered by a blow to the skull
it becomes disoriented, and, if bad enough, can make you appear dull."

"Now, I have a plan that will take advantage of your disorientation
can let you seek work far different from your previous vocation.
Where you've always worked hard
and dealt with animals and the elements,
this new job will be easier, safer,
and accommodate your minimal intelligence."

"What I have in mind actually capitalizes on your affliction
with your scrambled brain and your extremely poor diction.
With your scrambled brain, brought on by too many falls and kicks,
You have exactly what it takes to be successful in the world of politics!

THE EGG-SUCKIN' DOG

An egg-suckin' dog's
'bout the most useless animal is, they say
Lays around on the porch swattin' flies
And chasin' chickens the whole livelong day.

But, come nighttime when it's
Dark and quiet on the front porch stoop
His real talents come out and he's
More'n apt to be found in the chicken coop.

No, he's prob'ly not eatin' a neck,
Pulley bone, thigh, or a leg.
More'n apt, he's getting' up in the nest
and suckin' on an egg.

'cause, you see, when a hound gets a hankerin'
For those sweet morsels of yeller and white
They've started in a culinary direction
That's bound to seal their sad plight.

Anybody's ever had one
Knows what I'm talkin' about, I'll bet.
In fact, a friend of mine told me a story
That's one of the best ones yet.

He said one of his sister's aunts cousins
Told her husband, a man named Bobby Joe.
"Make up your mind—
Either me or that egg-suckin' dog's gotta go."

Now, I'll have to tell you the gospel's truth
That decision was a tough one, for ole Joe
'cause both her and the dog wuz pains in the neck
But, in the end, he decided the dog had to go.

We had one of those mutts on our farm when I was a kid
Got the hungries for the savory orb.
He started out quite innocently, but soon was
Eatin' as many as his stomach could absorb.

Now, our family loved eggs as much as he did
And his thievery just wasn't gonna do.
I knew from the look in my Dad's eyes
That the dog's days on our place were about through.

Sure 'nough, a week or two later
When I came home from school
The dog was gone; where I didn't know.
(I guess it was necessary, but it seemed sorta cruel.)

Of course, as bad as dogs suckin' eggs was,
What could really start your pulse to quicken
Was when the dog's poultry appetite
Turned from suckin' eggs to eatin' chicken.

Now, you've all seen the Chick-fil-A billboards:
"eat mor chiken," the skinny bovine pleads.
If a dog with a taste for domestic fowl sees it
That'll be 'bout all the incentive he needs.

So, if any of y' all are havin' any of these problems
With chicken-cravin', canine egg-eaters.
Do everything you can to not let them get a glimpse of
Chick-fil-A signs and, by all means start usin' Egg-Beaters!

BLUEBONNETS IN THE SNOW

What a strange sight, by morning's light
In our backyard San Saba space.
Ground covered in white; it snowed last night!
Brought a surprised smile to my face.

I never saw such a thing. Why, it's already Spring.
Doesn't the weatherman know
April 7th's the date; it doesn't snow this late.
No matter, it's sure snow!

There it was sure enough. Loads of the white, fluffy stuff
And the best part, you know.
Prettier than the rest, what I liked best
Was the sight of bluebonnets covered with snow!

The following are excerpts from the unpublished autobiography of a colleague of mine, Howard Hayre. He was born and grew up in rural Arkansas in the 1920's and 30's. As he relates, life "in the country" in those days had their light, halcyon, days but were also austere and hard. It's interesting to note that many of his experiences mirror those of others of his generation, regardless of the "country" in which they grew up. Watch closely as he relates vignettes about life in the rural South and how the people developed coping mechanisms by which they thrived, not just survived.

HOWARD HAYRE
(1924-)

The old house was gone by the time I can remember things like that. Dad built the house I grew up in. He made a "log" room about 12' by 14'(my guess). He hewed the logs to fit together. He covered the roof with wood shingles that he made by cutting a log up into about 14' lengths and then splitting out the shingles using a froe and a wooden mallet. A froe is a heavy knife with a handle sitting at 90 degrees to the blade. The log chunk is set up on end and the froe set sharp side down on the chunk at the point where the log is to be split for shingles about one-fourth. A hard blow with the wooden mallet splits off pieces inch thick.

He took rocks (which were plentiful around there) to use for a foundation. He used mud for mortar. He wrapped the walls with tar paper and used rolled roofing on the low pitched part of the roof. I mention all of this to try to convey the means he used to make a house as cheaply as he could. Mom wanted the inside walls to look better so she got wall paper and, using a flour paste for glue, put it on the walls. However, the mice ate that so she added some poison to the flour paste and solved the problem. Mom was quite ingenious.

Dad built a barn. It had a log interior room with sheds going out to the front and back, and it had a loft for hay. He built stanchions so he could have four cows at a time inside to milk, plus a stall for a couple of horses. A stanchion is a device made of wood in front of the manger. The animal puts its head in a position to eat out of the manger and an upright board can be moved into position so that the animal cannot remove its head back away from the manger. A feed box is placed in the manger to put some feed into, so the cow will be in position to be held in place for milking or for any other work that needs to be performed on her. A block is slipped in place to hold the upright part of the stanchion in place.

He built a hen house large enough to house about 100 hens. The outside walls of the henhouse were made of rock with mud for mortar. Now all of this was in place by the time I could remember. Of course we had an outhouse. It was about 50 yards back and to one side of the house. I can remember that on cold winter nights it was quite miserable to have to get up and go out there. We learned quite early in life to arrange to take care of those needs before going to bed.

From my earliest memories, we kept five or six milk cows, a few hogs to butcher each fall (after the first frost), and 50 to 100 laying hens. We had a cream separator, which was turned by hand, to separate the cream from the milk. We took the cream to town about once a week. We made cottage cheese with some of the milk:. That which we couldn't use, we fed to the pigs and chickens. The dog was fed table scraps. All potato peels and other scraps were fed to the pigs. Our water came from a spring at the bottom of a steep hill. I said it came from the spring, but actually it didn't come by itself. My brothers and I carried it up the hill in two and a half gallon buckets, usually a pail in each hand. Since my older sister, Henrietta, had housework to do, she was exempted from water carrying chores and getting wood.

Before I started to school, I was at home with Dad looking after me. One day in the winter while my siblings were at school, Dad had to go some place and left me by myself. Before he left he stoked the fire to keep the house warm. The stove was a "pot belly" stove that had a door at the front to adjust the air intake. He opened that little door, after he put in the wood, and went to do whatever—maybe he had to go to Wet Prairie to pick up Mom. Anyway, 1 had on my coat, but still wanted to get warmer. I backed up to the front of the stove and by an unlucky circumstance a spark from the fire popped out and my coat got on fire. When I realized what had happened, I ran outside and rolled in the snow. When 1 was asked later what I would have done if there hadn't been snow on the ground, I said, "I weckon I would have jumped in the wain bawel." (We kept a barrel or tub at the point where water ran off the roof. We used it for other things than for drinking.)

At the bottom of the hill behind our house and on down the hollow about 30 yards was our spring. It flowed a steady stream, winter and summer, wet or dry weather. At some time, a large tree had been cut and a piece about two and one half feet long was cut and hollowed out to a cylinder shape. A hole was dug where the spring came up and this "log" was put in the ground so that water flowed up and filled the cylinder and flowed out one side notched for this purpose. So when we went to get water we just dipped the bucket into the spring. The water was nice and cool. Most of the time we didn't cover the spring, except in the fall when the leaves fell.

Daddy built an area that could be covered where we could put milk in jars or crocks to keep it cool. We could also keep butter and cream there. This was important because we had no icebox. We often did the washing at the spring. We had an oval-shaped iron kettle in which we could heat water. We had a washing machine that had a handle that one could push back and forth to make the agitator work back and forth. We had a wringer that turned by hand to wring out the water. The advantage of washing at the spring was that we didn't have to carry the water up the hill, which was no small task when several tubfuls were required. It was an outdoor job anyway.

In the summertime, (my brother) Walter and I would sometimes go down to the spring to bathe. We would get a bucket of water out of the spring and slosh water on our bodies. Then we would soap and wash off. Then one of us would pour water on the other one's head. Cold water out of the spring is quite a shock and Walter could never stand still for it. I would start to pour it on him and he would turn and run and I would throw the whole bucket full on him.

When I was about nine or ten years old, Dad thought that I was old enough to look after the cows. Our place was fenced with barbed wire. It was cross-fenced to separate the fields that were farmed from the pasture. The barbed wire we used was made using two wires, about 10 gauge, twisted together with a barb about every 4 to 6 inches. This wire was strung out and stapled to wooden posts that were set in the ground about every 12 ft. The posts were made from trees from the woods. The posts were about 6 feet long and were set in the ground about one foot deep. Sometimes we would take a tree log and cut it to lengths and split it out for posts. Other times we would make the post from small trees, sharpening one end and driving them into the ground.

In the springtime, when school was "out," Dad would have me take the cows to the "Ward Place" and keep them there all day and bring them back about five o'clock in the evening. The Ward Place was an 80 acre tract of land which joined our north line. The Ward Place had no open fields. It was all hills and hollows. It had a stream of clean cold water running through it. The stream was fed by the Big Spring that was on the Murray Place. The Murray Place was the 40-acre place east of the Ward Place. No one lived on either the Ward Place or the Murray Place at this time. (The reason) Dad wanted to use this place for pasture was that in the early spring the grasses and clover started growing there and furnished pasture that we needed. Also our pasture was mostly woods and hills with the fields for farming cleared off. I would drive the cows down by the spring and on to our North fence.

At this point one might wonder why someone would need to stay with the herd all day! The Ward Place was not fenced! The cows could wander up the stream to the Murray Place and onto a road there that went on toward Sulphur Springs or back around toward the Pearce Place, or they could wander down the hollow to the Brown Place or on down the valley toward Sulphur Springs. Adjoining the north line of the Ward Place was another 80 acres that was also unoccupied. It was called the "Green Place." I suppose that someone named Green once lived there. There was a drilled well on this place, but it had not been used for a long time and was just a pipe sticking up out of the ground. I sometimes took the cows back there. My job was to keep the cows from wandering off and bring them back home in the evening. I was free to play in the stream climb trees, climb up on the rocks, look in the cave or do whatever interested me.

Think about what it would be like to be ten years old and be out in the woods by yourself! If you hurt yourself, no one is there to help you. If you get bit by a snake, what do you do? If the neighbor's bull gets out and comes into your herd, how do you deal with him?

"I SAW MERIDIAN FROM HERE"

A friend told me a story
About his Dad and a horse
It was so good, I thought I should
Share it with you, of course.

It seems the Dad
Was out rounding up some strays.
Riding his bay bounty way out in Bosque County
They were out in the boondocks a ways.

Making good time
They were goin' through a draw
A pretty rough ride, with cattle on both sides
Dad never knew what his cayuse saw.

One minute, fine
The next, upside down
Rain, although we're thankful, had the draw runnin' bankful
If Dad falls off, he'll drown.

What a sight!
That nag put on quite a show.
After a buckin' start, he came plumb apart
Where it'd end, no one could know.

Fishtailin' and snortin'
He was all over the place
He jumped so high he purt near touched the sky
A look of pure fear covered Dad's face.

Scared though he was
Ole Dad stayed right there on top
On top of all that, he never even lost his hat
He rode that bronc to a dead stop!

When it was over
Dad came out free and clear
When he landed, though it was miles away, I heard him say,
"I SAW MERIDIAN FROM HERE!"

A COWBOY AND HIS HORSE

The old matinee "shoot 'em ups"
Portrayed the cowboy in a strange way.
Didn't hanker much to women's work
And didn't have a whole lot to say.

When the purty young woman
Said something sweet to our ham
He'd just shuffle his feet, adjust his hat,
And say, "aw shucks, ma'am."

He'd never cast goo-goo eyes at 'er
Nor give her a loving glance.
Seems love was the last thing on his mind
Thinking, I guess, that he didn't stand a chance

To win her hand
Nor be the one for whom she'd fall.
So, rather than woo and lose,
He settled for not trying at all.

When the movie was over
Our hero rode off, of course.
Leaving the adoring damsel behind,
And him, sad-eyed, **kissing his horse!**

THE GREATEST OUTDOOR SHOW ON EARTH!

You call yourself the world's greatest anything
Sure as shootin' somebody's gonna call your bluff
'n you sure better be ready and willin'
To step up and show yore stuff.

But, those folks up in Calgary
Are right up there with that boast
Their rodeo's sure 'nuff
A good 'un…I'd say better'n most.

The rodeo brings in cowboys and girls
From places far and wide.
They compete for big, big bucks
And the biggest reward of all—cowboy pride.

The pride that goes with beatin' the best
Closin' in on the NFR
Showin' your pards and your fans
That you're among the best there are.

The chuckwagon races
Are a big part of the show.
Fast and reckless they fairly fly
And, at the finish line, lots of paper dough.

As great as it is, the rodeo's
Only part of the Greatest Outdoor Show.
There's fun, food, rides and stuff to see and buy
On the midway, exhibit hall, and the expanded casino.

Earl's deep-fried corny dogs—
The biggest and best you ever ate.
He's retirin' after this year's show
If you missed it, you're just too late!

So, if you're ever up Alberta way
Sometime around the middle of July
Drop on by Calgary, eh...
They call it The Greatest Outdoor Show on Earth
...and, mostly, them Canooks don't lie!

MURDER, ACCIDENT, OR SUICIDE?

Consider, if you will,
the case of poor ole Ron;
this boy just couldn't win, and in the end
he lost, but then again, he won.

The story goes a little like this:
Ron had had enough
he couldn't make it, just couldn't take it
his life had gone from smooth to rough.

So, we find him ten-stories up
getting ready to end it all
he's in the dumps, he's gonna jump
his life in a virtual free-fall.

So, we have a young man
who's reached a sorry state
he pauses on the verge, and with a final surge
he jumps—why more wait?

As he falls, he says to himself,
"I hope when I'm found
they find the suicide note I just now wrote
where I told 'em why I was so down."

On his way down
past the 9th floor he sped
a shotgun blast; the sound, his last
ere he hits the ground he's dead.

Now, here's where the tale
gets so weird it's apalling
below where he leapt, a safety net was kept
to protect workers from falling.

Hence, in the eyes of the law
he was murdered, not killed himself
as it all turned out, there was little doubt
he was killed by someone else.

A puzzling conundrum
the authorities now faced
the facts were confusing, certainly not one bit amusing
on which the case was to be based.

It happened that on that 9th floor
an old man and his wife were fighting
he grabbed his gun, put her on the run
when he shot he was off on his sighting

Instead of hitting her
the pellets went through the open pane
in lieu of her getting the lead, Ron got it in the head
so, we're back where we started again.

Under the provisions of the law,
"when one intends to kill subject 'A'
but instead kills subject 'B', then, by law, he
is guilty of killing subject 'B' so they say."

"But, we thought the gun was unloaded,"
says both the old man and his wife.
"We certainly would never, ever, ever,
intend to take another person's life.

"facts is," says he and she nods
"my threats to her are just sentimental.
I ain't never intended to have her life ended."
So, according to law the death is accidental.

Accidental, that is, if the gun
wasn't intended to be loaded with shot.
But, someone testified, the son had lied
they said he put shells in it likely as not.

Seems the old lady had done him in;
cut him off his financial dole
He then had a reason to commit this horrible treason
against his poor mother's soul.

The son knew what would happen
the next time the couple fought
the old man would feign to shoot her again
instead, it would result in the end he sought.

Hence, the son, who loaded the gun
should, by all things sacred by code
be held for the killing, for it's obvious he's willing
for his poor mom to get the full load.

The son, it was now clear
should be held for killing poor Ron
even though he didn't pull the trigger, it was easy to figger
he was guilty of the deed that was done.

Now, here's where the tale gets real weird
'cause ol' Ron was also the pair's offspring.
he was despondent from his failure to kill his mom
so he took the swan-dive to end the whole thing.

The shooting that followed
as he headed for the land
killed him, no doubt, but when it all filtered out
he was actually killed by his own hand.

So, in the final analysis
his murder, 'cause he done it himself
was part accidental homicide, part accidental suicide
but it couldn't be blamed on someone else.

Now, just remember this little saga
all you offending kids
don't you daren't try killin' yore pore parent
'cause you might get it in the end like Ron did.

THE COWBOY CODE

Cowboys have a code;
Their Golden Rules to live by
They shore wouldn't be bad'uns
For all us others to learn and try.

Try 'em on with me
See, they're simple and pure
Good rules for living
Proven, tried, and sure:

1.
Honesty is absolute
Yore word is yore bond, that's a fact
A handshake is more binding
That any written contract.

2.
Be there for a friend
That's a rule pure and true
Be there, day or night
Whenever yore friend needs you.

3.
Real cowboys are modest
He ain't ever all "gurgle and no guts"
He don't throw out his chest and brag
He knows that's just plain nuts.

4.

Be hospitable to strangers
Be nice to all as yore able
Even if'n they're an enemy
Make 'em welcome at yore table.

5.

Cowboys help them what's in need
Makes no diff'ernce who's hurtin'
Stranger, enemy, or whoever
Help 'em, pardner, for certain.

6.

Always say "Howdy"
To whoever you pass on yore way
It might'nt do nothing for him
But it'll shore brighten yore day.

7.

Don't put yore nose in nobody's past
It ain't yore bizness no way
Just take the measure of a man
For what he is today.

8.

A cowboy's pleasant
Even when he's got th' blues
Cowboys hate quitters
'n complainin' is what quitters do.

9.

A cowpoke don't go 'round
With a smoke in his hand
'cause he respects the environment
And don't want to burn up the land.

10.

Most of all, you'll find
That this last 'un is shore-nuff true
Cowboys respect themselves and others
And always live by the Golden Rule.

The world would be a much better place
As we ride on down the road
If cowpokes and city dudes alike
Lived and acted in line with the Cowboy Code.

THINGS I REMEMBER

A good friend of mine, and the father of another good friend and golf buddy, H.L. Crites, wrote the four poems that follow. H.L. died a few years ago and we miss him terribly. I've included Mr. Crites' poems not only for the wealth of insights into life in the country in Oklahoma in the early years of the 20th century, but as a tribute to his son, H.L. Mr. Crites was born on July 11, 1912 on a farm in Woodward County. The State of Oklahoma was only five years old at his birth. He was raised an only child on that farm, which had no electricity, telephone, or automobile. He walked to a one-room country school through the sixth grade, then transferred to public schools in Vici, OK, a town of 500 people. The town had dirt streets, wooden store fronts and wooden sidewalks with hitching posts. He remembers a livery stable to care for the horses that people had driven to town to do their shopping. He graduated from Vici High School and earned a B.S. degree in pharmacy from the University of Oklahoma in 1933. He worked as a pharmacist in small towns throughout Oklahoma until the end of World War II in 1945, at which time he moved his family to a larger community. He has a vivid memory of rural, farm and small town life from the World War I era through the great depression into the World War II era when things began to rapidly change into the present day lifestyle. Many of those memories are reflected in the poems which follow. It should be noted here that he didn't start writing poetry until he was well into his later years and one of his poems, "This Life—At Age Ninety," was recognized by the Oklahoma Department of Human Services, Aging Services Division, during the 2003 Oklahoma Conference on Aging. I am especially pleased to present a small sampling of Mr. Crites' works.

Memories of my early days
Bring me joy in many ways.
These are some I remember well
Some of the ones I love to tell.

Fresh fried chicken, home cured ham,
Homemade bread, jelly and jam.

Sitting on the creek bank, you and your dog
Quietly watching a frog on a log.

A cloudy day at the old fishing hole
Dangling a hook from my willow pole.

Running barefoot through the sandbur patch
Chasing a rabbit you are trying to catch.

On a hot summer day, a favorite story to tell,
Drinking cold water from the old oaken bucket right out of the well.

Out in the hayfield, early in the day,
Inhaling the smell of the new-mown hay.

Sleeping outside on a hot summer night,
Looking up at the moon, so big and bright.

Milking the cows, slopping the hogs,
Feeding the chickens, petting the dogs.

Walking each day to the one-room school,
Learning the basics and the Golden Rule.

Measles, chicken pox, mumps and croup,
All made well with Mother's chicken soup.

Reading a Zane Grey book by the coal oil lamp
Before going to bed or taking a nap.

Pumping enough water for the horses to drink,
Filling the stock-tank up to the brink.

Riding old Paint was a lot of fun,
Letting him walk or making him run.
Behind six head of mules, a long day of toil,
Riding the ridge buster, tilling the soil.

At the age of twelve, my first airplane ride
Looking down on the town and the countryside.

On a hot afternoon, dying of thirst,
Dropping a ripe watermelon, watching it burst,
Eating the heart and quenching your thirst.

Taking your girl to the show on her first date
And her Mother saying, "Don't stay out too late."

'possum hunting on a warm winter night,
under a full moon so big and bright.

The Saturday afternoon movie for a dime
A cheap way to enjoy two hours of time.

Your first kiss, you will never forget,
Oh what bliss! You remember it yet!

Apples and peaches, fresh off the tree,
A hot pie, made with cherries picked by me.

Rabbit hunting after a snow
Fun to do, a place to go.

Homemade ice cream on the Fourth of July,
Lots of fried chicken and fresh apple pie.

Teaching a newborn calf to drink
Out of a bucket is harder than you think.

Riding the Ferris Wheel with your girl
Holding her tight on the Tilt-a-Whirl.

Going to parties, playing games, sodas to drink,
Getting to know girls and how they think.

Ice cream on my birthday, a cake Mother made,
With enough ice left over for cold lemonade.

A nickel's worth of candy could always be had
If you went to town with your Dad.

Warm homemade bread, fresh churned butter and sandplum jelly
Sounds mighty good to a hungry belly.

These are some of the things that I remember yet,
Things that I will never forget.

DOWN BY THE CREEK

Down on the farm when I was a lad
Some of the best times that I ever had
Were when I was playing down by the creek
Day after day, week after week.

Wading in the water so warm and clear
Watching a frog on the bank so near
Seeing the minnows swim o'er the sand
Trying to catch them with my hand.

Using an old log for a seat
Feeling the warm sand beneath my feet
Sitting in the shade of the cottonwood tree
Seemed like being in Heaven to me.

The birds, the squirrels, hawks and bees
Enjoyed living in the nearby trees.
It was nature at its best
It was an ideal place to rest.

The grass was green on either bank
The cattle kept it from getting rank
They kept it eaten off so low
In the pasture, there was no need to mow.

Then there was the old fishing hole
Where I would dangle a hook from my willow pole
Sometimes I would catch some small fish
Which for my lunch became a savory dish.

That was more than eighty years ago
Most of a lifetime, this I know
I have never forgotten the good times that I had
Playing down by the creek when I was a lad.

How great it would be if I could go
Back in my life eighty years or so
And once again, play down by the creek
Day after day, week after week.

LIFE BACK THEN

How rural life has changed from long ago
The average person has no way to know.
One hundred-sixty acres is all you would need
To support your family and grow your feed.
Four or five horses, a couple of cows,
Some horse-drawn tools, a wagon, some plows.
A few chickens, a dog, maybe some sows,
Along with some seed is all you would need
To survive and succeed.

You never would pay for a neighborly deed
There always was help whenever a need.
You would help you neighbor harvest his crop
Or drop off his plow shears at the blacksmith shop.
You bought only what was needed and could pay for
Like a gallon of kerosene,
Bought for a dime at the grocery store.

The two-room house I grew up in
Was twelve by twenty four.
Four bare walls and nothing more.
A wood stove for cooking and heat,
No electricity, plumbing or toilet seat.
A coal oil lamp provided the light
To dispel the darkness of the night.
When in the summer it got too hot
We might sleep outside on a straw-tick or cot.
Water was pumped from a well close at hand

And kept in a bucket on a little stand.
Wash-pan and dipper were close by the pail,
With a towel always hanging on a handy nail.

I walked a mile and quarter to the one room school
Where I was taught the basics and Golden Rule.
In freezing weather, in rain or snow,
It was all the same, I had to go.
My dinner pail and a slate or book
Were the only things I usually took.
There I learned the basics of life,
Learned how to cope with troubles and strife.

Fresh apples, peaches and pears from the tree
A fresh cherry pie made just for me.
Fresh eggs from the hen house, honey from the bee,
Fresh churned butter, probably by me.
Fresh milk in the morning, homemade jelly and bread.
"That's mighty good eatin," has to be said.

Fresh from the garden, plenty to eat,
Peas, beans and potatoes, maybe even a beet,
Roasting ears right out of the patch
I just shucked and silked a new fresh batch.
Fresh tomatoes to slice and to can,
"That's mighty good eatin," man oh man!

We never went hungry, food always was good
Neighbors shared with neighbors whenever they could.
We always had meat to eat, chicken, beef or hog
And if there ever was any left, we fed to the dog.
This was living at its best, we raised every need,
Plenty of food for ourselves and for feed.

In the early days on the farm
Milk came from a cow
It didn't come in plastic jugs
Like we get it now.
Mother baked the bread
I churned the butter
The hens laid the eggs
And Dad squeezed the udder.
We let the milk set over night
'til the cream rose to the top.
Then we churned it into butter
And put the curd and whey in the Slop.

Up before breakfast, milked the cows,
Separated the cream, fed the horses,
Let out the chickens and slopped the sows.
Ate a big breakfast, steak, eggs and homemade bread,
Big cup of hot coffee, butter and jelly to spread.
Harnessed the horses for a long day in the field
Tilling the soil to produce a good yield.
The crop that is raised to feed and to sell
Depends on the rain and the weather as well.

A business deal made with a handshake never got wrote,
There was no need for a contract or note.
Your word was your bond, you did not kid.
If you said that you would, then that's what you did!

Such was the life lived back then
And a better life has never been.
Man has now moved on to a far different life.
One of hustle-bustle, confusion and strife.

The quest for gadgets that he does not need.
Takes all of his time and creates greed.
He is so busy, no time to live,
No time for others, no time to give.

Surrounded by crime, corruption and greed,
His main concern, his immediate need.
How sad it is that he cannot know
How great life was a few years ago.
If with this premise you don't agree
Remember, I have lived both lives.
I was there to see.

Would I go back? You bet I would!
Go back in a minute if I only could!
Back to when the work was hard and the days were long,
But you could end each one with a song.
Living in more simple times was a lot more fun,
Though a lot to do, you got it done.
No outside pressure, no locked doors,
Just the work of the day and doing the chores.
No silly gadgets to take up your time
No need to worry about theft or crime.
This is how I would love to live,
Having more time to live and give.

THAT TIME IN MY LIFE

Fifty-cent overalls, two-bit shirts
Calico dresses and gingham skirts.
Bright new blouses, worn with pride
Made from flour-sacks, bleached and dyed.

Baseball caps or stray hats
Homemade sunbonnets with cardboard slats.
These are the clothes that people wore
On Saturday to the grocery store.

Barefoot children, feet calloused and worn.
Having stepped on many a thorn.
The starting of school brought good news,
Always a pair of brand-new shoes.

You never bought things you did not need
Only flour and sugar and maybe some seed,
Coal oil, coffee and some dry beans,
Maybe some bacon if you had the means.
Money was scarce, you didn't have a lot
But you always paid for the things you got.

You might go over to the dry-goods store
For a spool of thread or something more,
Some yards of gingham and calico,
So that Mother might have some things to sew.

Some wealthy people, so it was said,
Had percale sheets on a feather-bed.
But flour-sack pillow cases and a cornhusk tick
For a lot of families, did the trick.

The crazy quilt was the family's pride
Usually pieced by the mother of the bride.
Made of scraps left from dresses and frocks,
Lovingly sewn into a pattern of blocks.
Quilted by church ladies with loving care,
Provided beauty, warmth and years of wear.

Such was life as we lived it then
And a better life seldom has been.
The work was hard and the days were long,
But we learned to cope if things went wrong.
A close knit community of neighbors and friends
All working together toward the same ends.
No locked doors, no fear of theft,
What was mine is yours if any is left.

Thank God that I lived at this time in my life
When I learned to cope with trouble and strife.
Where I learned to take and I learned to give,
But best of all, I learned to live.

OLD-TIME MEDICINES

Icthiol ointment
Pulled out lots of stickers
That black salve was easier
But a needle and tweezers were quicker.

Castor oil
Hadacol
Coaloil
Formulations designed to cure your ills
Rubbin' warts
Linaments of all sorts
Juices by the quarts
All kinds of salves, ointments, elixirs, and pills.

Remember when? Medicines back then
Were far different from today
Prescribed by Mom, they usually came from
The drug store 'round the corner or down the way.

Got a wart? The ugly sort?
Rub it with an old dishrag
Got a bad boil? Soak it in coaloil
It'll be gone 'fore your finger can wag.

Step on a thorn? Sure as you're born
There's Mom with the Ichthammol
Without a doubt, it'd draw that sucker right out
'n without the pain and blood and all.

Got a belly ache? There's lots of stuff to take
Try Syrup Pepsin or Carter's Little Liver Pills
Paragoric maybe, for the little baby
Enough alcohol and narcotics to cure all yore ills.

"Need doctorin'," the showman'd say.
"Try Nature's Own Way"
"We've got the purest of berries, barks, and buds."
Don't know if it'd cure anything, but it tasted good.

Whether you were stopped up or just simply achin'
There were plenty of "cure-alls" for the takin'
B.C. and Sloan's for pain,
Fatoff Obesity Cream for weight gain.

'though we're all sure those were good cures
we've got all kinds of new concoctions:
mycins and cillins, amines and statins
administered orally, inhaled, or by injections.

Are the new ways better?
Some of us are just not too shore.
They may cure as good as Mom's
But, they sure cost lots more.

And, you could get the old ones
Most times without a prescription
Lots were available over the drug store counter
Heck, you could even buy coaloil at the filling station.

BLINDSIDED!

Well, the trouble all started
When my father-in-law yelled, "Jack,
the old Brangus bull's out and we've
gotta go find him and bring 'im back
to the little patch up near the barn.
Git 'im back 'fore he runs plumb off
By then, he'll prob'ly want to eat
Outta his own feed trough.

Didn't seem like much of a task to me
'specially since I'd always been told
the old bull was feeble and near-dead
'cause he was so dad-gummed old.

Well, off to the Wagner pasture we went
Dad was purty shore that's where he'd head
The farther we went in that direction
The more the base of my neck tingled with dread.

'cause the weather didn't look much good
looked like the bottom could drop right out
shore as shootin', we'd be miles from home
when that cloud'd open up and drown us, no doubt.

We found that old scoundrel, just as I thought—
On the back side of the Wagner pasture, just a' grazin'
Wadn't givin' a hoot 'bout the weather comin' up.
Heck, he just went on eatin', just a' gazin'

at us as we rode up the trail toward him.
Prob'ly thinkin' "What in the world are they gonna do?"
Didn't seem too concerned with our welfare
Nor how hard we'd rode n' what we'd been through.

We gathered him up
And started back to the pens.
Tryin' hard to beat the clouds
'n the rain and worse therein.

We rode hard for most of an hour
Never stopped nor much slowed the pace.
The bull, he didn't protest too much
Just trudged along; resigned look on his face.

The rain had just started
When the pens finally came in sight
We covered the rest of the way quickly;
Me on the left and Pa on the right.

We were running at a high gallop
As we neared the last pen
"We got this thing wrapped up."
I thought…but the strangest thing happened just then…

All of a sudden, the bull turned hard to the left
Jumped hard right into my horse's right thigh
Wadn't nothing me or the horse could do
Just hit and roll and hope neither of us die.

I'm tellin' you that bull made a mess of us
The bull trampled both of us; the horse on top of me
My left leg felt like it was broke for sure
I didn't know what else I'd find if I ever got free.

Well, long story short, we got up
Both of us none too much the worse for wear
But the danged ole bull wadn't in the pen yet
'n I made up my mind we was gonna get him there!

So, after him we both went
This time, we didn't hesitate
I shore was glad when we finally
Got him in and closed the gate.

But, the ending of this story
Kinda has a funny twist
'cause I was bound and determined
to find out what it was I had missed.

"What happened back there
to make that ole rascal run plumb over me?
He just spooked so fast and hard
It's just something you seldom ever see."

"Well," said father-in-law, "it's this a'way.
I know'd you was hurt and you'd want'a know why.
That bull didn't even know you wuz there.
'cause, I forgot to tell you...
     that ole bull's blind as a bat in his left eye!"

TEJAS

The Caddo Indians had a word
Called "teysha," translated Tejas
In our language it's translated "hello friend"
And is the root word for our state, Texas.

Our state motto, "friendship"
Commits us in a certain kind of way
We are committed by dint of birth
To befriend someone new each day.

To go out of our way and do our best
To be friend to all who come our way
To raise our hands, say "Howdy"
As we go throughout our day.

Did you ever meet a pickup
And a feller stick up his index finger?
He's tellin' you "Hello" and "Good day"
And, if you have time, he'll stop and linger.

A while, visit, and pass the time of day
If'n you got the time, he might just invite you home
To eat a bite, visit with the Missus
Play "42" and hear a tune on the gramophone.

Need help? He'll be right there
Ready to help, whatever yore plight
A friend in need is a friend indeed
Whether hot or cold, day or night.

Yore hay truck's in a ditch?
Need help gittin' it out?
A friend'll be there lickety-split
'cause that's what friendship's all about.

Ya' gotta sick cow, no vet's around?
He'll be there with all his vettin' stuff
Why," some of you might ask.
I'd say, "most times just bein' a friend ain't enough."

Got a laid-up loved one, no family around
A friend will come over and sit
They know that you'd do the same thing
If and when it comes around to it.

Well, I've give you enough examples
Of what "teysha" means in Caddo talk
To us from around here, "a friend is one
Who talks the talk and also "walks the walk."

COUNTRY CADILLACS

Drive down any country road;
Go into any country town
One thing you'll find they have in common
Is how the folks there get around.

Some are old and dilapidated
Some are shiny, new and bright
They come in all shapes and colors:
Blue, green, red, black, and white.

Some call them trucks; I call them pickups
No matter what you choose to call 'em
When you've got things to do, they'll do 'em
When you've got stuff to haul, they'll haul 'em.

I'm talking about pickup trucks
The workhorse of the countryside
They're good for whatever you've got to do
They're the source of the country boy's pride.

2X4's, 4X4's, stepsides, customs, and duallies
They come in all speeds, shapes and sizes
"Tricked out," or off-the-showroom plain
In their owners' eyes, they're sure-nuff prizes.

We had lots of them when I was growing up
Starting with an old Ford, maybe about a '37
Atop a Sears catalogue, I started driving in that rig
It made me so proud; I was, you could say, in Hog Heaven!

Later, we got a '50 model blue Chevrolet
Maybe the only new one my Dad ever bought
I steered it with a steering wheel knob
And drove it faster than I probably ought.

On one such occasion, I remember it like yesterday
I was going home, down the road from the Lehman farm
Driving with my right hand on the knob
Out the window stuck my left arm.

Right at the corner was a bridge
Built over a rather deep little creek
Got my shirt sleeve caught on the knob
Headed into the hole—situation looking bleak.

Well, I missed the big hole, hit a smaller one
Had to get Mr. Lehman come pull me out.
Hoped he wouldn't tell my Dad
Or I'd be in deeper trouble, no doubt.

I guess he didn't, 'cause Dad never said anything
Anyway, I took that knob off and threw it away
It had already gotten me into enough trouble
Vowed I'd never have another after that fateful day.

One other pickup that I'll tell you about
It was the ugliest thing we ever had or I'd ever seen
A '53 model International ¾ ton monster
Yellow as a pumpkin, a real hard ridin' machine.

I drove it to Fort Worth many times
Taking pigs, sheep and cattle to the stockyards
Stop at a light, the thing wouldn't stay runnin'
People looking at me like I was a country retard.

I lived through it and don't seem to be much affected
'cept I still have to have a pickup as my ride
Even though I don't live on a farm or in the country
It's just an integral part of my old country pride.

So, wherever you are, whatever you do or drive
If, in your driving life, there seems to be a big lack
Just go down to your Chevy, Ford, or Dodge store
And buy yoreself a sure-nuff Country Cadillac!

A COWBOY DON'T…

A cowboy don't shirk from the kind of work
That cowboys are expected to do.
If there's work to be done, he'll be the one
You can count on to see it through.

Ridin' the fence line, throwin' his twine
Goin' from can see to can't see
He's never at a loss for anything on a hoss
He's as good a hand as ever could be.

I've seen 'em go through hell and snow
To save a dogie from the worst
Seen 'em go outta their way to save an old stray
Makin' sure some little orphan gets nursed.

Gotta horse that's lame, vettin's his game
He can bring 'em back to life
Calm and cool, don't need many tools
Just a rope and a fire and a sharp knife.

A cowboy don't lie, you want'a know why?
'cause his word's always his deed.
He lives by "the Code" as he rides down the road:
"A handshake's all you need."

But, for all the things a cowboy is and does
There's things a cowboy won't and don't do
I've got a hunch you, too, could name a bunch
But I'll start you off with just a few:

137

Now, a cowboy don't savor a coffee with "*flavor*."
He wants his tea cold, not hot.
He wants his tea cold, for bless his soul,
In summer's heat, it's all the coolness he's got.

A cowboy don't ever dress just to impress
"business casual's" not his dress style.
Jeans and boots and, in the winter, a union suit
And a denim shirt he's had for a while.

As good as he is, there's this code of his
He don't mulch, weed, or trim.
'n those of his ilk, don't gather eggs or milk
So just don't expect that stuff from him.

There's another thing, while I'm in that vein
That a cowboy don't hanker to do;
If you're talkin' domestic chores, his stops at the front door
He won't vacuum, dust, or "tidy up" for you.

Cleanin' the house, that's work he'll sure shirk
'cause the bunkhouse don't need much cleanin';
ask him to sweep, his silence he'll keep,
but, you'll sure know his meanin'.

There's lots more stuff, but you've had enough
to get the gist of my story.
What he does, he does hard, but be sure of this, pard
One thing a cowboy don't do much is worry!

The following vignettes are from an unpublished memoir penned by the mother of a friend of mine, Barbara Clark. Mrs. Merryman was a native Arkansan who lived most of her life in and around Van Buren and Conway Counties, the latter the site of Woolverton Mountain, made famous in a song written in 1962 by Claude King. Alice Merryman led a very colorful and rich life and it is chronicled colorfully in her memoir, which is concluded by the following poignant statement: *"So ends the tale that I have kept all of these years and I'm the only one of the group living. We did a good deed but it was also bad. I'm leaving it to God to be the Judge."* Please note the similarities between many of her experiences with those of my Mother-in-law, Norene Letbetter. Also, she and my Dad shared a commitment to education and both taught in country schools back in the 1920's and 30's.

ALICE DRIVER MERRYMAN (1906-2007)

I was born November 8, 1906 at Liberty Springs, Gridley Ark. in my Grandfather's log cabin. My Grandfather had built it after the Civil War.

I can remember when I first began helping my mother. She always depended on me and so did my Dad. He put me to plowing as soon as I could reach the plow handles. It was the team my Grandfather left us, "Buck & Sam," large mules. "Old Buck" was the slowest, laziest contrary mule I ever saw. It was probably the reason he lived so long. He must have been 25 or 30 years old when he kicked Woodrow in the face and split it wide open. A bad disfigure he carried with him to his grave. Believe it or not that mule lived until after I was married at almost 19 years of age.

We lived almost in sight of West Point Remove, which is now Driver Dam. The men had a swimming hole where they had a swing. We went in just our birthday suits to swim. Mama would take the girls and Papa would go up stream. She couldn't swim, but enjoyed trying.

I remembered going home with my Grandfather for the night. When the sun began to set, I cried to go home and convinced him I was very sick. He had Oda to saddle a mule to take me home. When he threw me behind the saddle, I busted out laughing. He said, "I have a great mind to take you down and wear you out." This wave of homesickness has never left me in all these years. When the sun begins to set, I long for home.

I learned many things by listening to the old folks talk. When my Dad was three, he and Aunt Betty were playing outside when a big wild sow came and took him by the shirt. It carried him away down the road, before Grandma could make it turn him loose. He was a very small for his age and grew very slow. My Grandmother was old when he was born and didn't give much milk. His sister Martha Jane who had a baby, Dora, (Orville Strouds mother), would walk half a mile every day to let him nurse.

They had many wild hogs even when I was small. They lived on acorns and hickory nuts. When there was a heavy crop they would soon forget to come home. They went wild and would sometimes attack people. They were hunted and killed. Much like other wild animals. Each person marked his hogs with a under bit or some piece cut out of their ears, every neighbor knowing his neighbors mark.

One preacher and his family by the name of Draper stayed with us 2 weeks or more. Mama said when they left she didn't have a frying size chicken on the place. During that time, it came a terrible flood and our crop was washed away. I had a bunch of goslings that I was so proud of and they all drowned. I cried and cried. Draper sang to me this song:

> Go tell Aunt Sally, Go tell Aunt Sally,
> Go Tell Aunt Sally her old Gray goose is dead.
> One she's been saving, One she's been saving,
> One she's been saving to make a feather bed.
> Old ganders weeping, Old ganders weeping,
> Old ganders weeping because his wife is dead.

He was a cruel man and we learned later a rascal.

One night they were having a meeting under a brush harbor with torch lights and lanterns. The babies and small children were on pallets on the ground when copper head snakes came to the lights. You never heard such jumping and screaming. It almost broke up the meeting. The preacher got them settled down and said it was the devil working in the form of snakes. A few nights later, the dogs had come to church with the wagons. Some boys caught them and poured high life on them. They ran right through the harbor screaming bloody murder.

One day as I was in the pasture looking for Buck and Sam (our mules) I spied a big hornets nest. I thought what fun it would be to put a rock through it. I couldn't have hit it more center. Here they came towards me. I ran for my life and laid down when I thought I was out of reach. One let me have it right on top of my head. Talk about headache, I felt like I had been hit with a sledge hammer.

In our growing up, most children got to make one trip a year to Morrilton. It was some 30 miles away. It was sort of a reward for our year of work. We took our cotton to market and bought a good supply of flour, sugar and coffee. Everything else we had to eat was raised at home.

On this trip we usually got one pair of "Brogan" shoes for winter and a bolt of cotton check dress material. Both the shoes and cloth were very coarse and heavy. Sometimes we got a bolt of flannelette to make our underwear. Until we were almost grown, Mama or Grandmother knitted our stockings. In the spring, Mama would make the trip to town and buy all of us a piece of material and make us a summer dress. Mine was always pink and Clara's blue. We always knew what we would wear, because we only had one Sunday dress. After we were larger we also got a summer hat.

We had doctors at Cleveland, 5 miles away and also at Scotland. They were Halbrook, Colay and Stover at Cleveland. Emmons and Hatchet at Scotland. They rode horses and came to our home when they were called. Their drugs were carried in Pill Pockets, a divided pouch thrown across the saddle. They went rain or shine. Many of times they never got as much as a "Thank You." Their drugs consisted of castor oil, caramel, paragon, morphine and lodium (quinine) for pain. You always got castor oil, a terrible dose, no matter what was wrong with you. You took quinine with a slippery substance wrapped around the quinine. This made it easier to swallow. We had a tree near our house that neighbors came to get the bark to make their remedy, known as a slippery elm tree.

They also had a "Mad Stone" which was a small stone from a white deer. Sometimes the stones were black but the white ones were more powerful. They derived their name from "mad dogs" which is now know as rabies. If you were bitten by a mad dog you went to where some one had a mad stone. It was soaked in sweet milk and placed on the bite and would stick for hours, turn green then soaked again until it was no longer green. Ed Smith was bitten by Olen Hunters dog and he used the mad stone. Never feeling any bad effects from the bites. But all of Olen's cattle and mule were bitten and went mad. I saw these cattle, they were very dangerous and tried with all their might to get to you. Their bawling and mooing was the most nerve shaking noise I ever heard. The mule went mad and he kept him in a log stable. You could stick a baseball bat through the crack and he would snap it into with his teeth. He finally bashed his brains out against the logs. It was always a question by neighbors why he didn't kill them instead of seeing them suffer. They died of thirst for when either human or animals smelled water they went into fits.

It was all a life at home program that you saved the ashes from the fireplace. You put them in a hopper to rot. In the Spring when the moon was shrinking, you poured water over the hopper and caught the lye at the bottom. You placed it in a large wash pot with some scrap hog meat and cooked until it made soap. You also took the lye and cooked with corn until tender and made hominy. We dressed and cured our own meat. Hog killing time was a day we all looked forward to—usually the first cold spell in November. By this time our meat supply was low or out altogether. We were all ready for a mess of spare ribs. Neighbors came into help and it was the custom to give them a good helping of spare ribs, backbones and liver. Here again the moon played an important part. If you killed when the moon was full, the meat swelled up and you could hardly render your lard. If you waited until the moon began to shrink and render your lard, you only have cracklings. The moon signs were also used in the planting of vegetables and crops.

We never had screen doors or windows, which was fine in the winter. In the summer flies, mosquitoes, dogs and cats had free entrance. Dad always loved cats and they were always a nuisance. One Sunday we were going to an all day meeting, Mama was packing her dinner in a trunk. When she had placed her last pie in, a cat jumped right in the middle of it. She threw it on the floor with all her might when it went into fits.

We went through a period of tick infestation. The law required that cattle be dipped. The state paid for the vats, which were built on concrete. They were barely wide enough for a cow to pass through. They were deep enough to cover their backs and about 15 or 20 feet long. These were filled with water and a solution to kill the ticks. The cattle were run through the vat, which had steps at the farthest end so the cattle could get out. We had to go out on the range and herd the cattle in every two weeks. Men were hired by the State or Country to go into each precinct and see that everyone was keeping the law. Feelings ran high. Many of the vats were blown to pieces before dipping day. My Dad was one of these men that carried guns and stayed prepared for any emergencies.

I still wanted to go to school and at 17 years old I went to Clinton High. I started in the 8th grade but was soon promoted to the ninth. I went there two years. I took the county examination and made a second grade teacher. My Dad got me a teaching job at Gridley School. I taught two months in the summer so that I would have money to go to school on that winter. Papa had captured some stills and the relatives had gotten together with the enemies and made it up to not send their children. They let me go on thinking that I was to teach. First day of school, I took my brother and sisters, but no one came. Uncle John Simpson came down and broke the news. I went home crying like my heart would break. The next summer I met some girls from Formosa and they told me I might get a school job at Culpepper Mountain. Papa objected to that and wouldn't let me have a horse to ride. So I started on foot, more determined than ever to make my way, to get out of that nest of relatives. I walked 10 miles to Scotland and caught a ride with Durward Burns to Culpepper. I got the school job at $45.00 a month, which seemed like a fortune to me.

BOW LAKE

Azure blue, mirror clear
Reflections bring the mountains near.
Snow-capped peaks' reflection
In the beautiful waters are nature's perfection.

Bow Lake by morning sunlight
Placid, clear, deep and bright.
One of Canada's most beautiful lakes
More beautiful without the wind's wakes.

Mountain peaks, capped with snow
In Bow Lake's waters their beauty show.
Pebbled bottom, in sun's light sheens
Adds depth and framework to the mountain scene.

Rugged mountains, a rocky collection
Seem strangely benign, in Bow Lake's reflection.
The juxtaposition of rugged and benign:
A key understanding of Bow Lake's design.

Try as one may, mere words cannot capture
The magnificence of Bow Lake's rapture
Adjectives fail the reader to conceive it
One must simply see it to believe it!

WORD GAMES

I got to thinkin' the other day
About words and phrases and how they've changed
Not just the way they're defined now
But how they've come to be arranged.

For instance, how many times has
Someone made a declaration that sounds to the ear
Like a question, 'cause at the end of t he sentence
The inflected question mark is all you hear?

But, the thing that bothers me more than that
Is the way we've changed the meaning of so many words.
As a result, in many conversations
You wonder just what it is you've heard.

For example, I overheard some guys talking the other day
It struck me as funny what they had to say.
I guessed they were discussing something that scared them
'cause they used the term "awesome" in a most exaggerated way.

But they weren't expressing Webster's definition of
Awesome: "A veneration shrouded in fear."
No, their use of the awesome word
Referred, instead, to the color of their hair!

How many times lately have you been in conversation
And someone kept saying, "He goes" or "she goes"
You looked to see the direction of their travel
Only to find out they're still there. Who knows?

I questioned after hearing that phrase the other day.
"Why say that when you're staying?" The reply, "Whatever."
Again, to Webster's book for clarification
And found no help there whatsoever.

Have you ever heard someone use the word, "like"?
Not in the Websterian sense: "to admire or revere"
But, in the hip sense, "Many, that's awesome"
And she replies, "Whatever."

A few more examples just occurred to me:
I heard the phrase, "Don't even go there."
Again, I looked around and wondered:
"Where?!?"

in this lingo, nothing is ever false
it is rather, "That is **soooo not true**."
Likewise, when something is, like awesome
More often than not it's **"way cool."**

Whatever happened to the good old days?
When language was so much more prosaic.
Words meant what they said and said what they meant
And sentences fit together in a linguistic mosaic.

I'm talking about poetic phrases like,
"Man, you're a real gone cat,"
"Ragg Mopp," and "Be-Bop-a-Lula"
and other meaningful utterings like that.

In retrospect, it may be that I misspoke.
Every generation has its unique ways of speaking.
So, man, it's like an awesome level of understanding
For which we all are seeking.

It matters less how that understanding is uttered
But how hard we work to interpret its meaning.
So, rather than shutting our ears to this new language
Listening for understanding would be a great beginning.

"YOUR BADGES, YOUR BADGES..."

They said it with a shrug, "we're looking for drugs"
They were DIA, ATF, and FBI
His name is Ed, he owns this ranch spread
And they're here and wants to know why.

"We need to inspect, because we have reason to suspect
that there might be illegal drugs here about.
"None here you'll find, but I shore don't mind
your turning my place inside out.

"but I'll have to be fair, don't go in that field over there."
Pulling his badge, the DEA guy says, "Bull,
we'll go where we want, our authority we'll flaunt
you've got the land, but we've got all the pull."

"O.K.," says Ed, that's all he said
He just looked again at the badge and the man.
The G-men were belligerent, but not at all intelligent
About the ways of ranching, cattle and the land.

He doesn't argue any more, just goes about his chores
Letting them go on their way.
So, when he hears all the screams, his old eyes just beam
'cause he knows what he'll hear them say:

"Get this bull off us, before he kills all of us.
Why didn't you tell us he was where we went?"
"I told you not to go, but in there you did so.
Don't blame me or the bull for your predicament."

149

"So, I've got one thing to say, before I leave for the day
'cause I see the old bull gaining step by step:
Your badges, show him your badges,
I'm sure they'll be lots of help!

THE CHANGING FACE OF CHRISTMAS

If you're anything like me
You probably remember with joy
How Christmases were when you
Were a little girl or boy.

When everything we saw
Was glowing shiny and bright
Where sounds of Christmas carols
Were pierced by shouts of delight.

Well, I'm feeling a little nostalgic
As we prepare for Christmas this year
It seems these feelings have increased
As my seventh decade nears.

Let me share with you some of the things
I think of at this time of year
Some may sound familiar 'cause
Some of you are my age or pretty near.

Remember huntin' for the tree
Ours came from the woods down the hill
Ax in hand, off we'd go
Looking for just the one to fit the bill.

Tree secured, next came the trimmin'
Lights, ornaments, and popcorn chains
Recyclable icicles, the star on top,
Tinsel rope, and loads of candy canes.

"Keep plenty of water in the stand,"
Mom would say, "or, it'll dry out and die."
That seemed to always be my job
'though I never knew quite why.

We just all had chores to do
My Dad, Mom and me
And, not all of them had to do
With getting and trimming the tree.

Mom, of course, cooked just the right things
Delicious bread pudding, mince and chocolate pies
Dad would bring home a Collins Street fruitcake
I actually liked them then, but I can't remember why.

Presents just seemed to materialize
Around and under the tree
Mom and Dad had clever ways
Of hiding mine from me.

It seems I had ways of finding them.
I recollect one year—I was 10 or so;
I found my favorite wish—a football.
I can play a while—they'll never know.

Well, as luck (and the Devil) would have it
I kicked it into a barbwire fence,
Ripped a big hole in it, couldn't hide it from Dad
And paid for it many months hence.

Christmas Days were spent at Mammy and Paw Paw's
Playing with cousins I rarely saw more than once a year
Lots of food, lots of playing, not big on gifts
But, filled with laughter, love, and cheer.

But, enough of this reminiscin' 'bout old times
After all, this is a poem about changing faces.
Christmases are so much different now than then
With the old only visible now in glimpses and traces.

Start with tree hunting in the pasture
Nobody does that kinda thing anymore
Now, we either go to the attic and get the fake tree
Or go down and buy a real one at the grocery store.

Trim a tree with popcorn and recyclable icicles?
Whoever heard of such a crazy thing?
Now, it's LED lights, crystal ornaments
Or, a tree that shines without a light string.

Presents, now that's what's really changed
Nowadays, the toys are so much more sophisticated
Wii's and X-boxes, dolls that do more things than humans
Anything you get now shows how it's voltage-rated.

So much about Christmas has changed!
As has the hectic pace we all seem to keep
Working and running from here to yon
Hardly having time to eat and sleep.

The things that haven't changed, though
Are those that mean the most to us
They're oft-times those that carry us through
All the hurry, bustle, running, and fuss.

We still enjoy having our family
Around us on Christmas Day
Allie, Jason, K.K. and Caroline
I enjoy just watching them play.

Of course, we all enjoy sharing
Food, presents, good times, and football
Watching the kids open their presents
But, through it all, most of all

The day still celebrates the birthday
Of the one born so long ago in Bethlehem
After all, when you cut through all the other stuff
We'd have nothing to celebrate but for him.

So, in that regard, it's important to remember
That He is still the reason we celebrate
That day, as the hubbub ensues around us
Pause a moment to consider this is, indeed, a
    Holy-date.

IN MEMORY OF GEORGE, THE WOODCARVER

The following poem is based on excerpts from an unpublished memoir of Mr. George Chiappini. I met George and his friend, Pat O'Toole, while attending the 2006 Arizona Cowboy Poetry Gathering. I learned that George was a very accomplished wood carver and was privileged to see pictures of several of his works of art. Subsequently, George and I shared e-mail messages and poetry over the next two-plus years. On one such occasion, I received a letter from him in which he enclosed the first two verses of a poem that he had started and which he wanted me to finish. That poem, "The Stampede" is one of my most cherished poems and is included in this book. On another occasion, he informed me that he had hand-printed (as was everything he sent me) his memoirs. He consented to send me a copy of it and the poem below is based on it. On April 7, 2008, I received an emotional e-mail from Pat in which she told me that George had died. I will miss him.

On a New Jersey dairy farm
George was born in 1919
The farmhouse, barns and pens
Were all parts of the family scene.

Like most farms of that time
George's had animals of all sort
Horses, chickens, and pigs
But, dairy cattle were the ones of most import.

Out near the pens
Was a great big manure pile
It was allowed to grow,
But had to be cleaned out after a while.

Then, the fun would start
All the boys got shovels and pitchforks
Then the…stuff would fly
They must'a had fun of all sorts.

One incident of that fun
From George to you I'll relate:
It gets a little gory,
So, please don't read after you've ate.

It seems the boys ran wild
Through woods on bare feet
One of the boys, Bill,
Was the fleetest of the fleet.

But, that day his luck didn't hold
Out he sang, "I cut my foot bad"
When the rest found him
They saw that he really had.

The little toe was dangling
Looked like it would come plumb off
George and Jess, though, "doctored" him
Thank Goodness, Bill was backwoods tough.

Long story short, they fixed him up
Sorta "stuck" the toe back on
And, after several days and weeks
By his Mom the truth was never known.

Boys, even back then, will be boys
Or, so the story goes and goes
George, in his memoirs,
Has related many more of those.

But, one last one, sorta captures
The life they led back then
It involves a snake, eggs, and nestlings
And recalls a time, when

A large black snake, like we've all seen
Raided a nest in a large solitary oak tree.
Try as hard as we might, he wouldn't move
But we just couldn't let him be.

We flailed at him with pole bean poles
'til we couldn't draw our breath
That old snake seemed to know
If he fell, it'd be to his death.

Finally, here comes cousin Al
He was older than the rest
And, being taller and older,
He could probably do the job best.

He addressed that danged snake
With cuss words and a bean pole
Finally, down came the snake
Bringing all the eggs and chicks he'd stole.

Well, Al wasn't ready to let the snake die
So, with more "colorful" words and the stick
(now, the rest of this might
just make some of you readers sick!)

Al put that snake on a hard surfaced road
And used that stick to roll him up
As he rolled out came...
You guessed it, Yup...

One chick, two chicks, three chicks
Out of that snake the fourth followed the third
Needless to say, the chicks were dead
But, Mr. Snake never had the stomach for another little bird!

AN OXYMORON:
UNRHYMING POETRY

A poem that doesn't rhyme!?!?
How on earth can that be?
Everybody knows a poem without rhyme
Is something else besides po-et-ry.

"Free verse," they call it
With skyward pointed nose.
"Free verse," says I
It ain't verse—it's PROSE.

Poetry's gotta rhyme
Ain't no doubt about it.
Rhyming words are essential to poetry
Words are just prose without it.

One thing songwriters are allowed to do
But us rhymin' poets ain't
Song lines can just sorta rhyme
Poetry lines can't.

We can't just throw out a long vowel sound
And hope they rhyme with another one
"lime" and "line" don't rhyme
neither does "some" and "done."

You really should work at your craft
If you're good, you should show it.
Readers expect your lines and words to rhyme
And believe me, they'll hear and know it.

So, if you're writing poetry
Let me tell you now so you'll know it
Be sure and make your lines rhyme
Or, don't expect me to call you a POET!

AN OLD FRIEND

"It's just an old red barn;
we oughta just tear it down.
Nobody lives here anymore.
They've all died off or gone to town."

"It takes money to keep it up,
what with taxes and paint and all.
Maybe we should just leave it alone
One day it'll get old enough to just fall."

Barns are kinda like that;
over time, like us, they get old.
The farms they service wear out
Or, worse yet, they get sold.

What good's an old barn if there's
no farm and farm folks around?
It just stands quietly out by the road
Silently overseeing the once-plowed ground.

I know of such a lonely barn
Once immaculate, stately and red.
Used for years by the Parks family
Most of whom are now gone or dead.

Since the early years of Wells County, Indiana
The barn has stood watch over Highway 224
The Parks' settled the farm many years ago
And husbanded the soil for eighty years or more.

George was probably born on the farm
And lived there most of his life
Even throughout his marriage
After he took Avis as his loving wife.

That barn has been steadfast through it all
The good years and the occasional lean
I remember the first time I ever saw it
I simply said, "It's the prettiest I've ever seen!"

Tall and majestic, a hay loft on top
Green roof, doors all trimmed in white
Cattle and hog shelters off to the side
Gleaming in the noonday snow—what a sight!

The Parks' barn, like others of its age and ilk;
built to serve the people, the stock and land;
built with love, care, sweat, and heart;
built strong to serve for years—built to stand.

But, paint fades and boards warp and rot.
Barns, like people, one day reach their end.
Years go by, we look back through pictures
And bid the barn a fond, "Good by, Old Friend."

.

COOKIE'S SPECIAL CHRISTMAS

Cookie says,
"I just can't hardly wait.
The bunkhouse is hummin', the parson's comin'.
I just hope he ain't late."

This Christmas's special
'cause it's Cookie's 60th year.
That's more'n most cooks make it; most just can't take it;
But, through it all, old Cookie's still here.

So, Cookie has planned
a visit the Parson'll remember.
He's bought presents galore, made grub and much more.
Been planning since way back in November.

"Let's see,
there's hay and grain for his horse,
a Bible edged in gold, a new slicker for the cold,
and a pair of new boots, of course."

The day's finally here.
Everything's prepared and in place.
Cookie's anticipating, he's growing tired of waiting.
But, so far, he's done it with grace.

Late in the afternoon,
A weak knock comes at his door.
"Oh dear, he's finally here.
My waitin's over for shore."

"Howdy Parson,"
Cookie greets his guest with a shout.
The door opens wide, "Well, bless my hide,
You ain't the parson, there ain't no doubt."

No, it warn't the parson;
instead, it was a little buckaroo.
He was dirty and scared, skinny and red-haired.
Surprised, Cookie says, "who are you?"

"My name's Joey.
I stay on a ranch called the Rockin' J.
My folks are all gone, I live on my own
But, I'm lost and can't find my way.

Touched, Cookie says,
"come on in, Joey, I'll fix you some hot grub.
My comp'ny ain't come yet, and I'm willin' to bet
You're hungrier'n a she bear with a new cub."

"Yes sir, I shore am."
After the food was blest,
he ate a meal fit for a king, with beef, taters and everything.
Cookie used the food he had bought for his guest.

After the boy left,
the weather began to deteriorate.
It commenced to snow, the north wind started to blow.
Cookie wondered how long he'd have to wait.

A second knock on the door.
Cookie jumped like he was shot.
His heart filled with glee, he thought, "this must be he."
But, opening the door, what a chill he got.

Again, it warn't the parson,
it was an old man with frost on his gray beard.
Cold and alone, no warm coat on his bones,
"He's shore near death," Cookie feared.

"Come in where it's warm,"
Cookie said without thinking.
"Yore needin' some chow; I've got a little left now"
Cookie's hopes for the parson now sinking.

The old man et
'til his hunger pangs abated.
"Now, sleep for a spell, leave when yore feelin' well."
With that, Cookie dozed and waited.

When the old man awoke,
Cookie sent him on his way.
But, this time with a slicker and boots, Cookie said, "shoot,
it's obvious the preacher ain't coming today."

Getting ready for bed,
Cookie heard a horse whinny outside.
Cookie thought, "oh dear, he's finally here."
Instead, it was just a splay-footed old hide.

Another shattered hope.
Cookie had to feed him, of course.
"I can't turn him away, I'll give him the hay
I bought for the parson's horse."

The horse, fed and sheltered,
Cookie returns, broken-hearted and sad.
He sat down in his chair, found the new Bible there.
He read to forget the day he'd had.

Somewhere during the reading,
Cookie fell sound asleep and dreamed.
He dreamed he saw the Lord and said, "I'd like a word."
"why didn't the day work out like I'd schemed?"

"I'd planned for days
for a nice visit with the preacher-man.
Bought gifts for him and hay for his horse. Now of course,
It's late and he's not coming as planned."

"My child,"
said the Lord, with care in his voice.
"the three came to your door, you gave what you had and more.
You gave freely because you had a choice."

"No," said Cookie
"I had no choice but to give.
I gave what I could, 'cause you said I should
That's how you taught me to live."

"Well learned," said the Lord.
Then, like a flash, He was gone.
Cookie knew without a doubt, when he sorted things out
It was good that he did what he'd done.

Cookie dreamed peacefully that night
Knowing that in its own way
Even though the preacher didn't come, the good things he'd done
Made this his most special ever Christmas Day!